Advance Praise for
❧ *What's in It for Me?* ☙

"In a story narrated by Rabbi Fuchs, a goat had horns so long that he could touch the stars. Then a man wished to use this starry quality for his personal purpose and took a little piece of the goat's horn. Soon others came with the same intent, and before long no horn was left. We must respect the goat. *What's in It for Me?* urges us to scrutinize our material needs in light of higher spiritual necessities. This book can be our faithful beautiful goat. Read and re-read it. Make it your companion. The title implies there is something for anyone. The moment I finished reading I knew what it is: an on-going refreshment of soul, an on-going Shabbat for everybody."

Anna Albano
Editor and translator
Milan, Italy

"...It was a joy to encounter Rabbi Stephen Fuchs' *What's in It for Me? Finding Ourselves in Biblical Narratives*. Rabbi Fuchs has given us a refreshing, practical application of how biblical stories may help us deal with the 21st century. Fuchs goes beyond the literalists battle over truth and historicity to mine these legends for the purpose that more enlightened elders used them: to help organize and inform daily life."

Michael Berkowitz
Consultant to the Government of China
In *The Huffington Post*

"I have been a Christian minister for more than 23 years and have found comfort on the path of interfaith service and understanding. This book written by Rabbi Stephen Fuchs is a gift for the soul of those who hunger and thirst for a deeper knowledge of God. It is not often we can sit at the feet of a wise one. Rabbi Fuchs has gained wisdom from his many years of service. His reflections in this volume teach us that faith leaves us with many questions and answers. As one sups with God while reading these pages rich with stories and reflections, we come to see the benefit of gathering with those who seek the Divine in different ways. The best gift is when one reads a book that makes them want to go back and study the "Good Book," all over again—with different eyes. This book is such a gift."

Rev. Dr. Shelley D. Best
President and CEO
The Conference of Churches
Hartford, CT

"Rabbi Stephen Fuchs invites us to take stock of our own lives, our perceptions and beliefs, as well as ownership of our actions. Inspired by biblical narratives, his book reminds us that we each have unique callings and the power to make choices that can make our world a better place. The variety in our beliefs, experiences and talents is what makes this world a beautiful and exciting place to call home."

Ana Cabán
Fitness, Wellness & Lifestyle Consultant
Certified Wellness Coach
Los Angeles, CA

"Reading this book is like taking a fully accessible walking tour through the Torah's grand narratives with a kind and learned tour guide at your side. Rabbi Fuchs' enlightened take on these ancient stories and their traditional commentaries offers us an interpretive lens that is rational yet passionate in its approach to God and Hebrew scripture. Throughout, the book invites us all—believers, doubters, and atheists alike—to take up the larger challenge of Torah, which is also the human challenge: how to make our world into the just, caring, and compassionate society we all seek."

Rabbi Debra Kassoff
Hebrew Union Congregation
Greenville, MS
Youth Education Director
Beth Israel Congregation
Jackson, MS

"Rabbi Stephen Fuchs' new book *What's in It for Me? Finding Ourselves in Biblical Narratives* is a culmination of a lifetime of study of biblical narratives that have shaped religious tradition. His interpretations of well-known—and some lesser known—biblical stories will appeal both to readers with deeply held religious beliefs and those with no belief system. In clear, readable prose, Fuchs presents cogent and understandable explanations of Biblical mythology and derives crucial lessons from the narratives. Many will find meaning and instruction in the teachings of this learned man and his texts."

Dr. Sally Wolff King
Senior Editor
The Emory Clinic
Emory University,
Atlanta, GA

"What's in It for Me? provides a clear and concise road map for living a more meaningful life. Rabbi Fuchs encourages us to make the world a better place, but does not stand in judgment of how we do it. There is something for everyone in this modern interpretation of ancient biblical stories, a deep and personal message to take on our own journey and pass on to future generations."

Laurie Kritzer
Executive Recruiter
West Hartford, CT

"You do not have to be religious to reap abundant pearls of wisdom from this book. It is accessible on so many levels because Rabbi Fuchs is able to take complex, confusing and abstract stories, explain their modern-day applicability, and weave them into a seamless narrative. The common thread that runs through them is the call to establish a just, caring, and compassionate society—to do what is right, productive, and positive by playing to our strengths. These lessons have certainly shaped my decision to be a mother, human rights lawyer, and social justice activist, and they imbue my life with fullness. We are fortunate that these lessons are now codified and available more widely in this remarkable gem of a book."

Jesselyn Radack
Director
National Security & Human Rights
Government Accountability Project

"I loved reading this book. Although I am a pastor and familiar with biblical stories and interpretations, I found a surprising connection to a new, deep insight or persuasive ethical impulse on every page. But it is not a Bible commentary. Rabbi Stephen Fuchs blends story telling and interpretation in a way that makes each chapter a little piece of art—beautiful and uplifting."

Rev. Ursula Sieg, Pastor,
Evangelical-Lutheran Church of North Germany
Bad Segeburg, Germany

"This is a book that transcends faith traditions and denominations. Wherever you are in your journey, this book will enhance your understanding. It is an important contribution to interfaith relations and conversations."

Rev. Damaris D. Whittaker
Minister
Center Church
First Church of Christ
Hartford, CT

"With insights gleaned from his forty years of work as a loving rabbi and an impassioned social justice activist, Rabbi Stephen Fuchs invites readers to see how biblical stories are relevant to and helpful for their daily lives. He makes a memorable case for why each of us should use our talents to forge a more just, caring, and compassionate society."

Dr. Kari Joy Winter,
Professor of American Studies
Director of the Institute for Research & Education
on Women & Gender
SUNY at Buffalo
Buffalo, NY

WHAT'S IN IT FOR ME?

Finding Ourselves in Biblical Narratives

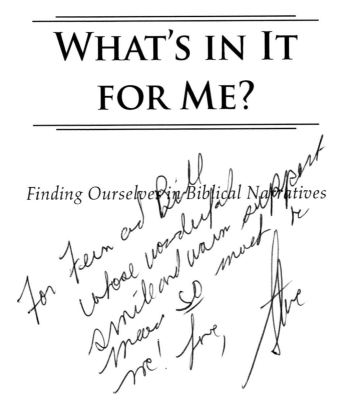

Stephen Lewis Fuchs

ISBN: 978-1-4276-5501-1

First Edition
First Printing

5774 —— 2014

Dedication

For Vickie
and for our children,
Leo, Sarah and Ben—

by far
my toughest critics and
from whom I have learned so much!

Stephen Lewis Fuchs

CONTENTS

Stephen Lewis Fuchs

FOREWORD

This is the story of the People of Israel as recounted in Genesis and Exodus, from the Creation to the edge of the Promised Land. In these pages, the author helps the reader find him or herself in the biblical narrative as one, who, like (Yisrael) Israel, struggles with God.

The truth in the overall narrative—and in the stories that compose it—is in this account primarily understood as moral truth. Rabbi Fuchs writes, "God of the Torah wants us to use our power to create a just, caring and compassionate society. We are in charge of and responsible for the earth. We have awesome power. We can use it for good or ill. We have free will. The choice is ours."

In the pages ahead, the reader will find many pastoral insights into how these texts pertain to daily life. These insights are shared in straightforward ways; gleaned from forty years of leadership and life with people in congregations, and many decades of study as Fuchs and the congregations he led interacted with and were shaped by Scripture.

One will also find that this text is not meant for Jews alone. The intent here is not narrowly pastoral but expansively so. It is explanatory in a way that reaches those who may not know the Hebrew Bible well. Readers of other faiths will benefit from Fuchs' considerable experience teaching, acting and interacting in countless interfaith settings.

Finally, the reader will find encouragement contained in these pages. Fuchs links the meaning of the texts to our concrete, contemporary lives, and shows us that each of us (believer or not) can, indeed, be who we are called to be. As Rabbi Fuchs says, "And even if we do not believe in God, we can choose life and blessing for ourselves and for others, and that is the choice that really matters."

Thus, as you read this book you will be informed, comforted, challenged and encouraged. But pay attention: For you may also find that in the process you have changed in important ways.

Heidi Hadsell, Ph.D.
President
Hartford Seminary
Hartford, Connecticut

PREFACE

This book is the result of more than forty years of thought, writing and revision. When I was a fifteen-year-old confirmation student, my rabbi, Avraham Soltes, of blessed memory, taught us that one of the marks of a mature person is the development of a personal philosophy of life. At the time, I had no idea of the true meaning of a "philosophy of life." Hopefully, at age sixty-eight, I do.

Simply stated: A good, caring God wants each of us to use our talents—whatever they may be—to make the world a better place. The biblical narratives I elucidate relate to this central idea. These narratives can enrich all of our lives whether we see ourselves as religious or not.

The project began in 1974, when the Baltimore Board of Rabbis, Conservative and Reform invited me to teach its area-wide Introduction to Judaism class for people contemplating conversion to Judaism or who were romantically involved although not contemplating conversion with a Jewish person. The course also welcomed Jews who felt their previous Jewish education was lacking.

While teaching this class, I found many adequate resources that explained the Holy Days and Festivals of Judaism and the various events of the Jewish life cycle. What I found lacking was a sufficiently concise and lucid presentation of the essential religious ideas that emanate from biblical narratives.

I filled that gap through my book, *What's in It for Me? Finding Ourselves in Biblical Narratives.* Further incentive to prepare this volume came in the late seventies when the Lutheran Theological

Seminary of Philadelphia invited me to teach an Introduction to Jewish Life and Thought course to students preparing to become Lutheran pastors. When I was granted a sabbatical in 1982 from my position as the first full-time rabbi of Temple Isaiah in Columbia, Maryland, my family and I lived in Jerusalem where I worked on this book in a more concentrated manner.

In 1988, while serving as Senior Rabbi of The Temple, Congregation Ohabai Sholom in Nashville, Tennessee, I began a four-year, part-time course of study at Vanderbilt University Divinity School leading to a Doctor of Ministry degree concentrating on biblical interpretation. My D.Min. dissertation was a text for the ceremony of confirmation with a creative liturgy based on the text. The service takes the congregation on a spiritual journey from creation to the revelation of Torah at Mount Sinai. The bulk of the dissertation was a thoroughly reworked and revised version of the text I had begun in 1974.

Since then, I have continued to review and revise my text and used it for classes I have taught at Hartford Seminary and the University of Saint Joseph in West Hartford, Connecticut. I have also presented it as gifts for comment and critique at several institutes for Christian clergy that I have conducted over the years.

And now, after yet more revisions, I am ready to offer it to nonfundamentalists eager to see how the narrative portions of the Torah relate directly to our lives today.

It is impossible to mention all of the people to whom I owe debts of gratitude over the long years this volume has percolated. I will mention a few and hope the rest will forgive me.

When I had all but given up hope, Susan Shuman of *SusanWritesPrecise* took an interest in this project and shepherded it through its final and most difficult stages of publication. Without her I don't think *What's in It for Me? Finding Ourselves in Biblical Narratives* would have seen the light of day.

I am grateful to Lisa Lenkiewicz for her editorial guidance; to Professor Kari Joy Winter for her many years of friendship and helpful suggestions; to Ruth Ann Harnisch who has, for many years, been there whenever I have turned to her for advice; and to Rabbis Beth Davidson, Michael Pincus, Harold Silver, and Charles Akiva Annes, z'l, and to Cantor Pamela Siskin. I extend warm thanks to Rachel Simon who shared valuable perspectives on the joys and sorrows of writing, to Anne Dubuisson for encouraging and guiding me through the often murky waters of preparing a book proposal, and to Janet Davenport for her expertise and patience as a copy editor. Thanks also to Nanam and Dustin at ECKO for all of their help.

The offers of Anna Albano and Pastor Ursula Sieg to translate this book into Italian and German, respectively, have shored up my confidence in its worth. I cannot thank them enough.

I owe an unpayable debt to my professors at Hebrew Union College, particularly Herbert Chanan Brichto, z'l, and Alexander Guttmann, z'l; at the Hebrew University of Jerusalem, in particular, Nehama Leibowitz, z'l, and Galit Hazan-Rokem; and at Vanderbilt University Divinity School, in particular James Barr, Walter Harrelson, z'l, and Doug Knight. I also cherish the special affection showered on me by my ulpan teacher in Jerusalem, Sarah Rothbard, z'l.

My greatest debt, though, is to the many students whom I have taught over the years and from whom I have learned so much.

Most of all I am grateful for the encouragement and support of my wife, Vickie, these past forty years. I cherish the love and support of my children: Leo and his wife Liz; Sarah and her husband Dan; and Ben and his bride-to-be, Kristin. My grandchildren Zachary, Micah, Jeremy, Noa and Flora are great blessings in my life. I pray that one day they will read and find meaning in this book.

Rabbi Stephen Lewis Fuchs
West Hartford, Connecticut
Erev Passover 5774

Introduction

The world today is seemingly divided when it comes to understanding the Bible. Religious fundamentalists hold that every word reflects unerring historical truth, while skeptics see biblical stories as little more than fairy tales. This book rejects both approaches. Rather, we view the Genesis and Exodus narratives as valuable instruction. Their truth is neither literal nor historical, but moral and ethical. Finding "truth" in a biblical narrative is akin to finding truth in a poem.

What does that mean? Let us say I am walking through a beautiful garden with my beloved on a gorgeous, warm spring afternoon. Overwhelmed by her beauty, I gaze at her and sigh, "Your eyes are two beautiful pools..." This does not mean I propose to dive in and take a swim, nor am I lying. I am, in fact, expressing a truth that rises from the very depth of my soul. I am presenting an accurate description of how my beloved makes me feel (Leonard Gardener et al., *Genesis: The Teacher's Guide,* New York: The United Synagogue Commission on Jewish Education, 1966, pp. 18-19). We turn to the Torah for enlightenment or personal guidance rather than lessons in science or history.

Torah is a Hebrew word that means "instruction" or "learning." It is a word that we understand in two ways: In its narrow sense, the Torah is the first five books of the Hebrew Bible: Genesis, Exodus, Leviticus, Numbers, and Deuteronomy. In a broader sense, though, the word Torah represents all of Jewish learning—all of the accumulated wisdom and teaching that through the ages, the Jewish people have contributed to benefit the entire world.

Overarching Jewish and Western religious thought is the magnificent story of Creation. Over the years, I have resisted recruiters' efforts to ensure the Genesis story of Creation is taught in conjunction with the theory of evolution in public schools. I resist because the biblical story of the Creation is not good science nor is it bad science. It is not science at all. It tells us absolutely nothing about *how* the world was created, but it offers invaluable insight as to *why*.

We do not read far into the Creation story before we discover the God presented in Genesis is different from the pagan deities worshipped by other societies. Genesis' God is not merely a powerful force whom worshippers seek to appease. The God of the Torah wants us to use our power to create a just, caring, and compassionate society. We human beings have godlike abilities, and the Almighty has set us in charge of, and responsible for, the earth. We have awesome power. We can use it for good or for ill. Since we have free will, the choice is ours.

Midrash is a form of Jewish religious literature necessary to understand how Jews read and understand Scripture. Midrash provides us with "corrective lenses" for our nearsightedness. In the Midrash (Bereshit Rabbah 8:11), we learn human beings stand midway between God and all of earth's other animals. Like the animals, we eat, sleep, drink, procreate, eliminate our waste, and die. But in a godlike way, we have the power to think, analyze, and shape the environment in a manner far beyond other creatures.

The message of the story is that God wants us to use our endowed gifts to establish a just, caring, and compassionate society on earth. But we—not God—must decide whether we will comply with God's wishes.

Stephen Lewis Fuchs

The concept of sacred time, which the Torah emphasizes again and again, is so central to biblical thought that it is woven into the very fabric of the Creation itself. If God is the force of good that we wish to emulate, and if God rests on the seventh day, then we should rest as well.

Our rest, though, is not just a time of relaxation and recreation. Our Shabbat is about spiritual rest. As the Torah tells us, it is a "refreshment of soul" (Exodus 31:17). It is a time for each of us to consider how we can use our God-given talents to create a better world.

Genesis 2:4 through Chapter 11 denotes three attempts by God to encourage us to live and act according to The Eternal One's wishes. The first attempt is in the Garden of Eden. Eden was a world of no birth, no death, a place where one did not have to work and, in my opinion, was devoid of sexuality. The first couple discovered their sexual capabilities only after they ate of the Tree of Knowledge.

After Eden, God established a second society with new ground rules. We became sexual, procreated, worked hard, and died. As it turned out, the second society also failed. Cain killed Abel and everything unraveled. Finally, God floods the earth and chooses Noah—"a righteous man in his age" (Genesis 6:9)—to survive the flood and rebuild the world.

Unfortunately, the third society gets off to a horrible start and ended with the story of the Tower of Babel. From a modern perspective, I am moved by the story of the Tower of Babel because it answers the question non-Jews ask me most frequently (second only to "Why do Jews not believe in Jesus?"). That question is: "Why do we have to have all these different religions? Wouldn't the world be better if there was one religion instead of all the problems caused by religious differences?"

My response to the question if the asker is a Christian is, "Whose religion would it be? Would it be yours, where the life, death on the cross, resurrection, and ascension to heaven of Jesus are the guiding beliefs and set of religious principles? Or would it be mine, in which the life and death of Jesus plays no role whatsoever?"

No. Religious unity should not be our goal. Rather, respect for, and appreciation of honest religious differences is what will lead us to a better world.

Through the Midrashic lens, we understand that society number three was no better than numbers one and two, and now God has a serious dilemma. God still cares. God is still disappointed in the lack of moral progress of the world. Nevertheless, God has promised never to destroy the earth again.

There is an answer to the dilemma. God chooses Abraham, Sarah, and their descendants with whom to enter a sacred covenant. In that covenant, God promises to protect us, give us children, make us a permanent people, and allot us the land of Israel. However one feels about the Middle East today, make no mistake the Jewish connection to that piece of land traces to the very beginning of our story as a people.

A covenant is a bilateral agreement. In return for God's promises, God charges Abraham's descendants to:

- "Be a blessing" (Genesis 12:2).

- "Walk in God's ways and be (my translation of the Hebrew word *tamim* is) worthy" (Genesis 17:1).

- Fill the world with and teach your children to practice "righteousness and justice *(tzedakah* and *mishpat)*" (Genesis 18:19).

Perhaps the most noteworthy feature of the God of the covenant is that God enters into a true partnership with Abraham and his descendants, and as we later see, we can influence and even inspire the Almighty!

What a concept. Our actions can influence God! We are charged to fill the world today with righteousness and justice, just as God charged Abraham and Sarah with that responsibility 4,000 years ago. However, we all have free will and can use our talents as we see fit.

Today, three great religious traditions identify Abraham as our spiritual father. We share many common ideals and goals. Yet we also have genuine religious differences. As twenty-first-century seekers of harmony, we must not simply tolerate but understand, respect, and affirm our differences. Hopefully, whether we practice Judaism, Christianity, or Islam, or any other religion we can find inspiration in the ancient hope that God not only cares about the choices we make, but is moved when we act righteously in the quest to redeem our troubled world.

The journey through the biblical narratives from the Creation to Mount Sinai and beyond can be the most important journey we undertake. In these stories, people of any or no belief system can find inspiration and meaning.

Stephen Lewis Fuchs

CHAPTER I

Creation: Religious—Not Scientific—Instruction

The Creation story in Genesis is one of the most misunderstood stories in all of literature. No narrative better illustrates the dichotomy between those who interpret the Bible literally and those who dismiss it as quaint folklore.

Clearly, the story is not scientific. C'mon! A big light to rule the day and a little light to rule the night...a heavenly firmament with water above and floodgates that open to cause a deluge? No, the Genesis Creation story is not good science. It is not bad science. It is not science at all. It is an exquisitely instructive religious poem.

The Creation story in Genesis tells us nothing about *how* the world was created, but it tells us so much about *why* the world was created. It is hard to imagine so short a story containing so much valuable guidance. Unique among the creation stories of the ancient world, the Genesis story presents a good, caring God whose desire is that humans establish a just, caring, compassionate society on earth. Everything about the Creation poem is purposeful and orderly. If life on earth is created with purpose, then we can conclude that *our* lives have purpose too. The rhythm and cadence of the language in the story, even in English translation, contribute to this focused theme.

The method of creation is simple declaration. God says, "Let there be...and there was..." The pattern continues until the creation of humanity. Then, the language changes dramatically. If the poem were a musical composition, the music would change too.

Suddenly, instead of "Let there be," we find, "Let us create humanity in our image after our likeness...and they shall take responsibility for the fish of the sea, the birds of the air and everything that creeps on earth. And God created humanity in the image of God, male and female, God created them." (Genesis 1:26). What a profound statement. It does not mean that we look like God because God has no form or shape. Rather, it means that we, above all creatures on earth, are the most godlike. We alone have the power to shape the environment and the fabric of our society for better or for worse. We are the only creatures who can go to a mountain, mine ore from that mountain, and turn that ore into iron, the iron, into steel, and the steel into the most delicate of instruments with which to perform brain surgery. But we are also the only creatures that can mine the same ore, turn it into iron and turn that iron into steel to make bombs and bullets—whose only purpose is to kill or to maim! What awesome power we have. The crucial question the Creation story asks us is how will we use it? Will we apply the talents we possess for good, or for ill? The choice is ours, and the responsibility is ours, as well.

A famous Midrash teaches when God finished creating the world, the Almighty addressed humanity, saying, "You are in charge of and are responsible for this earth. But it is the only one you will get. So preserve and enhance it. Do not pollute or destroy it" (Kohelet Rabbah, Chapter 7). Sound advice for us today.

In the late eighties when then Tennessee Senator Albert Gore, Jr. began his campaign of environmental awareness (which led to his receiving the Nobel Prize for Peace in 2007), he asked me to prepare "a closing homily" for the first meeting of the initiative held in Nashville, the city where I then served as rabbi. On that occasion, I related a venerable Hasidic story told in many different ways about a magnificent goat that lived long ago. The goat had horns so long and beautiful that when he lifted his head, he could touch the stars, and they would sing the most beautiful melody that anyone had ever heard.

One day, a man was walking through the forest thinking of what he might give his wife for her birthday. He encountered the goat, and a brilliant idea jumped into his head. "I could make my wife a gorgeous jewelry box from a piece of one of the goat's horns," he thought.

The man approached the goat, which was very tame and friendly, and explained, "I want to make a jewelry box from just a small piece of one of your horns. It won't hurt when I cut it off, and I'll just take a small piece. You won't even miss it!" The goat lowered his head to accommodate the man's request.

The jewelry box that the man fashioned was indeed beautiful, and his wife adored it. Proudly, she showed it to all of her friends who soon wanted one just like it. You can see where this is going. Soon the goat was inundated with requests to "cut off just a small piece" of one of his horns. Of course, soon his horns were much shorter. The goat could no longer reach the stars, and that most beautiful melody was forever silenced.

This wonderful tale teaches one of the vital lessons of Genesis' Creation story. We, human beings—not the crocodile, the elephant nor the lion, though they are stronger, faster, and fiercer—are in charge of, and responsible for, this world. Therefore, if we are to pass on a beautiful and healthful environment to our children and grandchildren, we must do a much better job than we are doing now of taking care of it.

The Creation story also introduces one of the most important of all Jewish teachings: Shabbat, the Sabbath. This story introduces the wonderful idea (see Thomas Cahill's best seller *The Gifts of the Jews*) that there are two different types of time: ordinary time and sacred time. We need ordinary time to do our work, go to school, produce, and achieve. But we also have sacred time to ponder why we do what we do and what the meaning of our lives can be. We are not robotic automatons—at least we should not be—simply going from one day to the next with mindless functionality. We need sacred time—the Sabbath—to consider who we are and what *our* talents can do to enhance, rather than tear down the divine image in which we are created.

Hopefully, by now, we can see the Creation story *neither* as history nor science *nor* as a fairy tale. The story opens the Bible to teach us that life has purpose and meaning. We, and not the rhinoceros nor the tiger, are in charge of and are responsible for this earth. It is an awesome responsibility, and to remind us that we need—once each week—a day that is different. We need a day to step back, breathe deeply, rest, and ask ourselves, "How am I using the talent with which God has blessed me? How can I do a better job?"

CHAPTER II

Eden: Would You Want to Live There?

The first society God established was the Garden of Eden. Eden was a place of no birth and no death. There was no need to work hard, and there was no understanding of our capacity for sexual expression and procreation. Only after they ate from the fruit of the Tree of Knowledge did the first couple discover these aspects of life.

The story of Eden is one of the most famous in all of literature. We can look at it in (at least) three distinct ways: from the standpoint of classical Christianity, classical Judaism, and a more modern view, which I propose and recommend.

For classical Christianity, Eden represents nothing less than the Fall of Man. We had it made. God provided for all of our needs in the garden and asked only that we not eat from one tree. We disobeyed, plunging humanity into a state of sinfulness. God sent His only son, Jesus, (if and only if we believe in him) to redeem us from the sinful state into which we are all born, and to promise us eternal salvation.

Jews, of course, do *not* believe this. Traditional Judaism considers eating the fruit of the Tree of Knowledge a wrongdoing for which there have been consequences. Specifically, we must work hard for a living, childbirth is painful, yet, our fundamental relationship with God remains unaltered. Jesus plays no role in our salvation.

There is a third way—and to my mind, a most instructive way—to view the story. Eden was a nice place to visit, but not to live, precisely because Eden was a place of no birth, no death and no sexuality. Eve is not the villain of the story, but the heroine. She is not interested in an endless life of ease without challenge or purpose. Although she did not know what life outside the garden would be like, she was willing to risk the uncertainty for the possibility of a life filled with meaningful achievement, satisfying relationships, and the ability to bring new life into the world. She was eager to abandon life as it was in Eden, even if it meant that her life span would have a limited duration. I relate to her decision.

After a long year of work, few things seem more attractive than the prospect of an Eden—lying on a beach with clear water lapping at my toes; fresh ripe fruits hanging above my head, ready to pick and eat. Certainly, there are no cigarette butts anywhere.

Yes, that would be paradise, and I would love to be there... for about a week. Maybe after a particularly tough year, I would sign up for ten days. After that, I would seek out a challenge that would bring meaning to my life. That is how I imagine Eve felt when she chose to eat the fruit. We should see Eve as a truly heroic figure whose bold action inspired God to create a new society in which a meaningful life is not only possible, but encouraged.

Knowing we will die is neither punishment nor curse. It is a call to us to make each day as meaningful as we can. None of us knows when our lives will end. Therefore, we should waste no opportunities to use our talents in a positive, productive manner.

Stephen Lewis Fuchs

Seen this way, the story of Eden is not the Fall of Man, but the elevation of humanity.

Whichever way one interprets the story, Eden as a society did not succeed. Therefore, God establishes a second society with new ground rules. In this new society, people have sex, work hard and die.

Stephen Lewis Fuchs

CHAPTER III

Cain and Abel: "The Symbol Story of the Human Soul"

God's second attempt at encouraging humanity to establish a just, caring, and compassionate society begins with the famous story of Cain and Abel. No story in literature teaches us more about what God is—and what God is not—than Cain and Abel. Two brothers make offerings to the Lord: God accepts Abel's and rejects Cain's! Why? Jewish tradition has been uncomfortable with the idea that the Eternal One would act capriciously. So the consensus of Midrashic thought is that Cain brought an ordinary offering or, perhaps, an insultingly inferior one. Abel, on the other hand, brought the best offering he could.

When we read the text this way, it is clear why God accepts Abel's offering and rejects Cain's. But I do not think that this is what the text is saying! The crucial verse (as I translate it) reads, "In the course of time, Cain brought an offering to the Lord from the fruit of the soil, and Abel also brought the choicest of the firstlings of his flock" (Genesis 4:3). In other words, each one brought the best he could. Furthermore, the initiative to make an offering in the first place came from Cain, not Abel.

But if we read the text that way, we grapple with a difficult question: Why does God reject Cain's offering? It does not seem fair. And isn't God all about fairness? The answer is simple: We do not know. God is a mystery, and life is not always fair. God does not answer to us. We answer to God. We lose sight of this at our peril.

Moreover, the Torah does not always tell us the way things should be. Sometimes it underscores the way things are. In daily life, we all make offerings—even our very best offerings—that those in a position of power reject as God rejected Cain's.

Did you ever study for days for a test in school and got a C+ while smarty-pants Harriet just thumbed through the book in homeroom before the exam and got an A? How did you feel? Did you ever practice and practice and practice to make a team and wound up on the far end of the bench while someone who did not practice nearly as long or as hard as you became a starter or even a star? Have you ever applied to a college or university and got a thin envelope with a letter thanking you for your interest but saying that due to the high number of qualified applicants, the school is unable to accept you? Have you ever primed yourself for a certain job or a promotion that went to someone who you knew in your heart was less qualified than you were? Have you ever offered your love to one who did not feel the same about you? Yes, we all have been in Cain's shoes. When we are, we too are angry at and jealous of smarty-pants Harriet, the guy who starred on the team, the people who got into our first-choice college, the less-qualified applicant who got the job, and the one who walked off with the person we loved. Without doubt, we all have been in Cain's shoes—and often.

What happens in the story teaches us so much. God takes time out of (what we presume is) a busy divine schedule to speak one-on-one with Cain. "Surely, if you do right, there is uplift," the Eternal One encourages him (Genesis 4:7). God is saying to Cain then, and to us now, "I know how you feel. I even know what you are thinking. Don't do it. Hang in there. Keep trying." To try our best and to keep trying is the ultimate measure of success! In the end, doing our best is more important measure than a teacher's grade, a coach's evaluation, a college's decision to accept or reject an application or a new job or promotion. If we give every situation our best effort, we learn and grow from our mistakes. And then we have achieved true success. It is one of life's most important lessons and one of the most difficult to learn.

Nevertheless, even after this one-on-one conversation, even after God makes clear what would happen unless he bridled his anger and jealousy, Cain killed his brother! This teaches us the concept of free will. Indeed, life would be meaningless if we were only puppets with God as the puppeteer.

In short, the story of Cain and Abel teaches us what God is and what God is not better than any story ever written. God is the voice of our conscience urging us to do what is just and right, what is productive and positive. But—and this "but" is huge— God does not make us do anything. So if Cain was determined to ignore God's voice and kill Abel, God does not prevent him from doing so.

How profound a point is that? Perhaps the question people have asked me most frequently (perhaps even more frequently than, "Why don't you Jews believe in Jesus?") is, "Why didn't God stop the Holocaust?" My answer is, "Read Cain and Abel." The fourth chapter of the first book of the Torah instructs us not to expect God to stop holocausts or any other act of evil. God exhorts Cain and us not to make rash and foolish decisions, but God does not stop us from making them. Often, I wish God would intervene, but then if God did, the lives we live and the choices we make would lack meaning.

After Cain kills Abel, God asks, "Where is Abel, your brother?"

And in the voice of a petulant child, Cain answers, "I don't know. Am I my brother's keeper?" (Genesis 4:9). God's answer rings out across the millennia: "Of course you are!" That is the whole point. If God's goal in creating the world is for human beings to create a just, caring, and compassionate society, then the only way to achieve that goal is if we assume responsibility to be our brother's or our sister's keeper.

The story of Cain and Abel is truly profound. In sixteen short sentences, the Torah teaches us some of life's most significant truths. Nobel laureate John Steinbeck considered *East of Eden* (an 800-page expansion on the Cain and Abel theme) his greatest work. Steinbeck called Cain and Abel "the symbol story of the human soul because it is every man's story." We all face rejection many times in our lives. The toughest question and most important question we face is how do we deal with it?

CHAPTER IV

Noah: The Purposeful Choice
of a Purposeful God

"All too familiar and easily dismissed" is an apt description of the biblical story of Noah and the flood. Academics consider it just one of many ancient Near Eastern flood myths. However, they miss the point. Yes, there were other stories of floods in the literature of the ancient Near East, and the Noah story is arguably the latest of them. But the differences between Noah and the other stories of floods are far more significant than their similarities.

Only in the biblical flood story does a good, caring God cause a deluge. This is because God grows weary of humanity's inability or unwillingness to do what the Almighty wants us most to do: create a just, caring, and compassionate society on earth. Only in the biblical flood story does God choose the hero explicitly because "he was a righteous man in his age" who "walked with God" (Genesis 6:9).

The Talmud (B. Sanhedrin 108a) records an interesting argument between two sages. Rabbi Yohanan claimed God considered Noah righteous only because everyone else at the time was immoral. Resh Lakish contends Noah's goodness is all the more praiseworthy precisely *because* everyone else was so unscrupulous. Thus, Noah had to overcome the negative influence of the surrounding culture.

I posit a contemporary situation for my students in college and seminary classes to identify with Rabbi Yohanan's and Resh Lakish's argument. I ask them to think of themselves as an admissions officer for a college or university. On the last day of applications, with only one place left in the incoming class, two students apply. Alice is a strong student from a very good high school with lots of AP classes under her belt. She has high College Board scores and is involved in many extracurricular activities. The other applicant is Ruth. She is valedictorian of her inner city high school. Her Board scores are 175 points lower than Alice's scores and she has no time for extracurricular activities because she works after school to help support her family. Which student is more worthy of that last spot in the class? Rabbi Yohanan would vote for Alice and Resh Lakish for Ruth.

The flood ends God's second attempt to have humanity establish a workable society. Both the idyllic Eden as well as the post-Eden world have failed. Yet, God does not give up. After the flood, God begins again with three new ground rules.

In the post-flood society, for the first time, God gives humanity permission to eat meat (Genesis 9:3). Personally speaking, I decided to adopt a nearly vegan lifestyle because my studies of Genesis' earliest chapters lead me to believe that is the way God wanted humans to live. The permission God grants us to eat meat after the flood seems to be a grudging concession to human nature. In so many ways, I believe, our world would be a better place if we did not raise and slaughter animals for human consumption. Aside from the vital question of compassion for other living creatures, we would all be healthier with plant-based diets, and the impact on our eco-system would be enormously positive if we all adopted a vegan lifestyle. I strongly believe that we would come closer to living up to the responsibility we have as creatures created in the divine image if we did not slaughter animals for food. (For a more thorough discussion of this topic, please see my chapter titled "Enhancing the Divine Image" in *The Animal Ethics Reader* (Susan Jean Armstrong and Richard George Botzler, eds., Taylor and Francis London (second edition), 2008, chapter 36).

In the second change from the pre-flood society, God charges humanity with the responsibility for setting up a system to administer justice (Genesis 9:6). We, not God, are now responsible for punishing wrongdoers.

The third new ground rule is that God promises never again to destroy the earth because of anything humanity might do. The message is clear: We might destroy the earth, and there are those who contend that we are well on our way by our neglect or warlike actions, but God will not (Genesis 8:21 – 22). The awesome power that God granted humanity at the time of creation becomes much greater after the flood. The aftermath of the biblical flood story is an ideal place to begin a discourse that explores our responsibilities toward the world in which we live.

CHAPTER V

The Tower of Babel: God Opts for Diversity

The Third Society—the post-flood society—unfortunately gets off to a horrible start. Fresh off the ark Noah gets drunk. His son, Ham commits disrespectful acts (or much worse, according to Midrashic accounts) toward his father (Genesis 9:21-25). Humanity tries to rebel against God by building the Tower of Babel (Genesis 11). The biblical text does not make clear precisely what happened to make God so angry with the builders of the Tower of Babel, but the Rabbis of the Midrash saw the tower as a rebellion against God (Bereshit Rabbah 38:7). According to another Midrash, *Pirke de Rabbi Eliezer* (Jerusalem, Eshkol, pp. 78-79, and *Midrash Ha-Gadol* 11:3), the wickedness of that generation was so great and their disregard for human life so extreme that if a brick fell from a scaffold, all work would stop until the brick was retrieved and placed back in the tower. If, however, a person fell from a scaffold, that was no big deal. They would simply plaster over the injured person and build him into the tower.

People often ask me why we don't have a single religion instead of so many different ones that cause so much conflict. The conflicts are not the result of different religions. I believe they are the result of our unwillingness to accept religions different from our own. While I am a passionate Reform Jew, I do not believe that everyone should be Jewish. I am so fond of the Tower of Babel story because it affirms the value of diversity of both language and belief. After all, God created diversity by scattering people and creating different religions, languages, and cultures. How can this diversity be anything but a blessing? (See my discussion of the Tower of Babel in the Introduction on pages xv-xvi).

Nevertheless, the rebellion of Babel is a clear sign of post-flood society's failure. Now God indeed has a dilemma. In short, God is dissatisfied with humanity's actions, God still cares deeply about the world, but God has promised never again to destroy the world. God responds to this dilemma by making a covenant with a single family that would change the course of human history.

CHAPTER VI

Abraham: God's Covenantal Partner

God makes a covenant with Abraham, Sarah, and their descendants. In this covenant, which is the basis of all of Jewish thought, God promises four things:

1. To protect Abraham

2. To give him children

3. To make his descendants a permanent people

4. To grant him and his descendants the Land of Israel

But, and this is crucial, we do not receive these things for nothing. In return, God charges Abraham, and all of us to whom the covenant speaks, with three very specific responsibilities that we must fulfill:

1. "Be a blessing" (Genesis 12:2).

2. "Walk in My ways and be worthy" (Genesis 17:1).

3. "Keep the way of the Eternal One by doing what is just and right" (Genesis 18:16).

The chapters in Genesis describing Abraham's life (Chapters 12-25) are not a complete biography. Rather, they are a series of highlights that speak to how Abraham endeavored to uphold his end of the covenant. In that regard, they soar across the millennia as instructions to us. We will examine four examples.

When God announced the destruction of Sodom and Gomorrah, Abraham protested mightily, "Shall not the Judge of all the earth do justly?" (Genesis 18:25). Abraham was calling God to account for a perceived lack of the very justice and righteousness that the Almighty charged him and his descendants to uphold. Patiently, though, God lets Abraham bargain (are there fifty, forty-five, forty, thirty, twenty, ten righteous people there?). Finally, Abraham understands that Sodom and Gomorrah were without any righteous residents, except Abraham's nephew Lot and his family.

From the standpoint of Midrash, Abraham's protest is even more astounding. Without changing a letter, the Hebrew version of the question, "Shall not the Judge of all the earth do justly?" can be changed to a statement, "The judge of all the earth shall not do justly." (Bereshit Rabbah 39:6)

The meaning of this change is profound. Abraham is arguing that the Almighty has to "lighten up" a bit. God has already pronounced three societies (Eden, post-Eden through pre-flood, and post-flood) failures. Abraham implores his Maker: "God, if You ever want society to work, then You cannot insist on such strict standards of justice." You have to be more understanding of human frailty. You have to temper justice with mercy." By patiently allowing Abraham to protest, God allows Abraham to see for himself that Sodom and Gomorrah had *no* righteous people in the cities worth saving.

Because of his protest and God's forbearance with it, Abraham realizes, finally, that God is just and that he can have faith in God's instructions. That certainty of the trust that God earned is crucial to our understanding of the story we shall discuss next.

Our second example involves one of Scripture's most puzzling and profound stories, the near sacrifice of Isaac. How, we wonder, could God ask such a thing? How could Abraham agree? Why does Abraham, who stood up to God and protested mightily on behalf of the strangers in Sodom and Gomorrah, not object when God instructs him: "Take your son...whom you love, Isaac, and offer him as a sacrifice on one of the heights that I will point out to you" (Genesis 22:3).

The answer is that after his argument with God over Sodom and Gomorrah Abraham knew God was just and knew that he could trust the Almighty even when God asked him to do something seemingly unthinkable: Sacrifice his own son. Some interpreters assert that by taking Isaac to Mount Moriah, Abraham failed God's test. Others opine that while he might have been a great religious leader, he was a failure as a father to Isaac and a husband to Sarah. How else, they ask, could a good man be willing to sacrifice his own son? I contend, respectfully, they miss the point.

Human sacrifice was the principal scourge of the pagan world to which the new covenantal religion objected. The new religion that evolved into Judaism completely rejected human sacrifice. It is that horrific practice, which, I submit, the story of the Binding of Isaac decries. In beckoning Abraham to Mount Moriah to slay his son, but staying his hand, God sends a message that humanity still struggles with today. No civilized religion can accept human sacrifice in its name. From the ancient world out of which the covenant emerged, to the Spartans of ancient Greece, the Incas, Aztecs, Mayan, and Hawaiian civilizations of other hemispheres, pagan religion has always involved human sacrifice.

Indeed, a serious student of the Bible understands that the perceived efficacy of this horrific form of human behavior was difficult to uproot from the mindset of the ancient Hebrews as well. No fewer than fifteen times does the Hebrew Bible protest human sacrifice or cast it in a shameful light. Does a parent ever tell a child not to do something fifteen times when the parent has no worry whatsoever that the child will do that thing in the first place? Of course, not!

No biblical story illustrates how difficult it was to convince our ancestors that human sacrifice was an abomination better than the story of Mesha, King of Moab (ca. 850 BCE). Mesha had paid tribute to King Ahab of Israel, but rebelled after Ahab's death. In the ensuing battle, the Israelites were routing the Moabite forces until (in the words of the Israelite biblical author), "Seeing that the battle was going against him, the King of Moab...took his firstborn son and offered him up on the wall as a burnt offering. A great wrath came upon Israel, so they withdrew from him and went back to their own land" (2 Kings 3:25-27). The point of this amazing story is that the biblical author clearly believed that Mesha's act of human sacrifice is what turned the tide of battle in his favor.

When we evaluate the revolution in human thought that the God of the Hebrew Bible represents, I contend that the absolute rejection of human sacrifice is even more significant than the insistence on one God as opposed to many gods and the rejection of idol worship!

Critics of Abraham's behavior in the story of the Binding of Isaac point out that God never again addressed Abraham directly after the incident. So what? This does not change the reality that Abraham remained God's active covenantal partner until the end of his days. His acts of covenantal responsibility at the end of his life were every bit as significant as those earlier in his covenantal career.

Why did God ask such a thing of Abraham? And why was Abraham willing to do it? God and Abraham had a unique relationship, which illustrated a brand new way of experiencing God to the world. Unlike the pagan gods, God in the Torah is not simply a force to appease. Rather, God is the source of moral and ethical values that brought a much higher level of civil thinking to the world. One of the vilest aspects of the pagan world was human sacrifice. It is befitting, then, that God and God's unique covenantal partner, Abraham, should present a dramatic demonstration to the world that human sacrifice should never occur. That is why God could ask Abraham to do the unthinkable. That is why Abraham, who protested so forcefully for the sake of strangers in Sodom and Gomorrah, so willingly complied with God's request.

Suppose for a moment a parent called me and said, "Rabbi, you will not be seeing Petunia in religious school anymore because this morning, God told me to take her to the mountains and offer her as a sacrifice." Naturally, I would do everything possible to convince the parent that the voice he or she heard was not that of God. Moreover, I would do everything, including notifying the police, to stop him or her from doing this.

Of course, the scenario I just proposed is absurd. Nevertheless, we have yet to learn *not* to sacrifice our children. It happens all the time. It happens each time we send our children to fight wars over conflicts that could better be settled by negotiation. It happens each time we force our children into pursuits or professions to satisfy our own ego's needs. It happens every time we overwhelm our children with pressure to succeed, never letting them feel that they are good enough.

The great British entertainer Lena Zavaroni (1963-1999) is a case in point. Born on the tiny Scottish Isle of Bute, Lena Zavaroni was an amazing musical talent with a magnificent voice and boundless charisma and charm. As a little girl, her aunt whisked her off to London to pursue fame and fortune. She achieved both in spades. By the time she was ten years old, she had appeared on *The Johnny Carson Show,* toured Japan, and sung for Queen Elizabeth and President Gerald Ford. By the end of her teenage years, she had starred in three successful British TV variety series. She was the highest-paid entertainer in the United Kingdom. View her *YouTube* video clips. She was amazing.

Ah, but when she was still a young girl, people began to tell her that she looked a bit pudgy. To make a long, sad story short, Lena Zavaroni—once the richest teenager in the world, adored by millions—died broke and penniless from complications of anorexia at age thirty-five.

Beautiful, precious Lena Zavaroni was every bit as much a human sacrifice as Jephtha's daughter (and the rabbis of the Midrash condemn Jephtha as a fool) in Chapter 11 of the book of Judges. Every time I watch her sing, I want to reach into the computer screen, hug her and promise, "I won't let anyone hurt you!" But it is a promise I could never make, let alone keep. And Lena Zavaroni, who appeared thinner and thinner with each passing year of her young life, is just one of millions of examples of horrific human sacrifice we have offered throughout the centuries and continue to offer today.

Yet many contemporary rabbis and others bemoan the fact that God asked Abraham to sacrifice his son. They just don't get it! They just don't get that God and Abraham tried to teach the world a vital lesson—a lesson we still have not learned.

According to Midrashic tradition, Abraham endured ten most difficult trials in his career. The sages note, the only time Abraham wept is when his beloved Sarah dies. Commenting on her age of 127, we read Sarah died with the wisdom of one who had lived a hundred years, retained the beauty of a woman of twenty, and the youthful exuberance of a seven-year-old (Bereshit Rabbah 58:1). After Sarah dies (Genesis 23), Abraham seizes the opportunity to gain an undisputed toehold in the Promised Land by paying an exorbitant price for her gravesite. God promised Abraham and his descendants the land, but Abraham is never a passive covenantal partner. Proactively, he does all he can to ensure that God's promise comes true.

On its surface, the scene is ridiculous. Whoever heard of the need to convene all of the elders of a community, from the governor on down, to witness the simple purchase of a burial plot? Nevertheless, this is exactly what Abraham does. He wants the sale to be public knowledge so there will be no doubt of its legitimacy.

Do not be fooled by Ephron's offer to "give Abraham the land." That was standard bargaining procedure in the ancient world. When he named his price (400 shekels of silver), Ephron surely expected Abraham to dicker and bargain. That is the way things were done back then (and largely, that is the way they are done today, to which anyone who has shopped in the old city of Jerusalem can attest). But Abraham was having none of it. To Ephron's shock, Abraham does not dicker at all. In plain sight of the whole community, he weighs out the 400 shekels and turns them over to Ephron.

Why the elaborate procedure? Why is Abraham willing to pay what historians of the period agree was an outrageous price for a burial site in a cave? The answer is simple. There were laws covering contracts in the ancient world, but as a noncitizen, or resident alien, Abraham did not benefit from the laws' protection. (We see this phenomenon in the story of Jacob, when Laban breaches his contract with Jacob over the marriage of Rachel and then violates the clearly stipulated laws of Haran concerning Jacob's service as his shepherd.) Perhaps the greatest legal innovation from Torah law—aside, of course, from its insistence on God as the force demanding justice and righteousness of humanity—is for the first time in the ancient world, the laws protected non-citizens. More than any other precept, 36 times to be exact, the Torah emphasizes that the stranger shall enjoy the same protection under the law as citizens in ancient Israel "because we were strangers in the land of Egypt and we know the feelings of the stranger" (Exodus 23:9).

The final chapter in Abraham's career deals with finding a wife for Isaac (Genesis 24). The stakes were high. The very future of the covenant with God was on the line. Abraham calls his senior servant, who clearly understands how vital the task is, and makes two conditions:

1. No Canaanites for my son because the Canaanite values were completely removed from the covenantal ideals of justice, caring, and compassion.

2. Return to the land of Haran from which I migrated. Find the right girl and bring her here.

Unquestionably, Abraham wanted the servant to find someone with "covenantal potential," someone who exhibited the values of caring and compassion on which The Covenant was based.

The servant (whom Midrashic tradition unanimously claims is Eliezer of Genesis, Chapter 15) asked Abraham a logical question: "What if the 'right' woman won't follow me here? Shall I take your son Isaac back to the land from which you came?"

Abraham answered unequivocally: "Absolutely not! In fact if the girl will not follow you here, you are free from this oath" (Genesis 24:8). Why was Abraham so adamant about this? Because if Isaac went back to Haran, Abraham might just as well never have left and made his historic journey toward a new ways of life in the first place! If Isaac goes back to Haran, the fledgling covenant would be in mortal danger. The only way he could guarantee its continuity was for the servant to find the covenantally suitable woman in Haran and bring her into the "covenantal incubator" that Abraham had established in Canaan.

As he waited by the well, the servant devised the perfect test. When he asked a maiden for a drink, the woman who not only obliged but who also offered to water his ten camels would be the one! After all only a woman of kindness and compassion would offer to work as hard as watering ten camels (of a stranger no less) would require.

Rebecca, as we shall, see is perceptive and capable as well as hard working. She emerges as the strongest personality among the biblical matriarchs, and her husband Isaac plays a secondary role to her in the narrative.

Rebecca, not Isaac (Genesis 25:23), heard from God that her younger son, Jacob, not her older son, Esau, would be the covenantal heir. Like Abraham, she does not simply rely on divine promises. She makes things happen. When her husband is old and blind, he is about to pass the covenantal blessing to Esau (Genesis 27:5-13). While her ethics are questionable, her vision is clear. She senses that it would be disastrous for Esau to receive the blessing and convinces Jacob to follow her plan to obtain it for himself. Afterward, when Jacob has reason to fear retribution from Esau, Rebecca devises the plan that saves him (Genesis 27:41-46).

Like many other women later in the Bible (Tamar, Zipporah, Yocheved, Deborah, Hannah, and Samson's unnamed mother), she is much more in tune with God's will than her husband is. In bringing Rebecca from Haran to wed Isaac, Abraham's servant not only fulfills the oath he makes to Abraham, he ensures covenantal continuity.

Chapter VII

Jacob: Is this the One to Inherit The Covenant?

Jacob is the most complex character in Genesis. His story is fundamental to our understanding the message of the book. Jacob is a disagreeable boy. He extorts the family birthright from his hungry brother. He stands before his blind father and lies twice, claiming to be Esau. Finally, he steals the blessing Isaac plans to give to his older brother (Genesis 25 and 27).

The birthright and the blessing are two different things. The birthright is the economic benefit the first-born son received. Upon the death of the father, the first-born received a double share of the family estate. In the case of Isaac, Esau would have inherited two-thirds and Jacob one-third of the family property and assets. If there were three sons, the oldest would receive half and the other two a quarter each. It is as though there were an extra son and the eldest received the extra share. The birthright also made the eldest son responsible for taking care of his mother and sisters upon the death of his father. The birthright is what Esau sold away for "a mess of pottage" (Genesis 25:34).

The blessing that Jacob steals in Chapter 27 is completely different. The blessing conferred—on the one who received it—direct responsibility for carrying on the Covenant that God made with Abraham. Isaac wanted to give Esau the blessing, but Rebecca convinced Jacob to steal it. Many years ago in an *ulpan* (an intensive Hebrew language course in Israel), I criticized Jacob for the horrible things he did to his brother. An Orthodox woman in the class (verbally) jumped all over me. "How can you be so stupid?" she spat. "Don't you know that Esau was a brigand and a murderer and Jacob was a Torah-studying *Tzaddik* (righteous man)?" She, of course, was quoting Midrash, which to her is literally true. Although I love Midrash, I quarrel with the viewpoint it presents that Jacob was righteous and Esau was wicked. These interpretations are a rabbinic invention to justify God's choice of Jacob over his older brother as the covenantal heir.

As in the story of Cain and Abel, the rabbis are not comfortable with the notion that God might act capriciously or in a way that seems unjust. In these two stories, Midrashim do not amplify the reader's understanding of the biblical text. They inhibit it. They lose sight of the cardinal rule of interpretation that a biblical text can never lose its plain straightforward meaning. In the Bible, there can be no doubt that Esau is the innocent victim of his brother's chicanery. We must acknowledge, without vilifying Esau, that Jacob had more latent covenantal talent than his older twin. Though he had many character flaws, Jacob was quite capable of future planning and big-picture thinking.

As for Esau, many years ago, a Bar Mitzvah student of mine, David Broida, pegged him perfectly: "Esau was not bad. He was like a boy who, if offered a whole chocolate cake right now or a ten-speed bicycle later, would choose the chocolate cake."

Yes, *rabbinic* literature may justify Jacob, but *the biblical text itself* better describes the nuance and subtlety of the man. Repeatedly, the Bible judges Jacob's actions harshly, and he suffers severe punishments for his grievous sins.

Consider this: Laban tricks Jacob in the same way Jacob tricked his father. Jacob, the younger, substituted himself for his older brother when his father could not see. Laban turns the tables by substituting the older sister (Leah) for the younger (Rachel) when Jacob could not see. It could not be more symmetrical (Genesis 29:16 ff.).

Jacob married four women, but the only one he really loved (again, Rachel) was barren (Genesis 29:31). After finally being able to conceive, she dies while giving birth to her second son (Genesis 35:18). His daughter Dinah suffers a humiliating rape (Genesis 34). His son Reuben sleeps with his father's concubine (Genesis 35:22), and his favorite son, Joseph, is kidnapped and presumed dead (Genesis 37). In biblical terms, each of these events in Jacob's life can be viewed as a punishment for his youthful indiscretions. In addition, Jacob lived his final seventeen years dependent on his son Joseph for sustenance (Genesis 47 ff.).

Laban's act of tricking Jacob by substituting Leah for Rachel in the bridal canopy was just the beginning of Jacob's twenty-year sentence at what I refer to as, "The Laban Reformatory of Hard Knocks." Laban made Jacob's life a living hell. As Jacob noted, "These twenty years I spent in your service, you held me responsible for every animal lost to marauding beasts. Scorching heat ravaged me by day and frost by night. Sleep fled from my eyes, and you changed my wages time and time again..." (Genesis 31:38-41).

Until the day he left home to escape Esau's wrath, Jacob had lived with no thought for anything or anyone beyond his own selfish desires. His moral horizons began to broaden the first night he is on his own. In his dream, God repeats to him the covenantal promises the Almighty made to Abraham. When he awoke from his epiphany, Jacob exclaimed, "Surely the Eternal One is in this place, but I did not know it" (Genesis 28:16).

As Jacob grew in wealth, he grew in humility and perspective. However, 20 years of exile were all Jacob could endure. He decided to travel home even though he knew Esau had vowed to kill him and was on his way to meet him with a regiment of 400 men. As he prayed to God for help, Jacob acknowledged that he was "unworthy of all the kindness" that God had showed him (Genesis 32:11).

On the night before he met his brother, Jacob struggled with everything he had been and hoped to be. It was a life-altering struggle. After he wrestled with God, his conscience, and all he had done to Esau, he emerged a new man with new determination. He resolved to reconcile with Esau and to ensure they could cooperatively coexist—each in his own land. He also limped on an injured hip to teach us that truly coming to grips with God—and the way God wants us to live—involves pain as well as progress and reward.

With whom did Jacob struggle on that eventful night? Was it an angel, his conscience, or did he struggle with God? Perhaps it was the spirit of his brother Esau, or a combination of the above. We cannot be sure. We *can* be sure that after the struggle, Jacob awoke a new man with a new name. He became Israel, which means "one who struggles with God." Only after that night did Jacob begin to realize his full potential as a covenantal partner with the Almighty.

Note that the name Israel does not mean to believe in God or to understand everything about God. It means to struggle with the idea that despite all the evil and immorality we see in the world, there is a good, caring God who implores us to use our talents to make the world a better place. The invitation to that struggle—to find the way each of us can use our talents to make a better world—emerges from the Hebrew Bible, but is open to all of us whether we identify with a particular religion or not.

After the struggle, Jacob knew that Esau prepared to wage war (Genesis 32:7), but he prepared to make peace. He sent his brother a generous offering (Genesis 32)—an abundance of cows, bulls, goats, camels, ewes, rams, and donkeys. Through this gesture, Jacob endeavored to return to his brother the material value of the birthright he had wrested from him long ago (Genesis 25:29).

With this offer Jacob, who is now Israel, was saying, "I acknowledge and regret the pain I caused you." The gift was so substantial and so sincere that by the time Esau and Jacob met, Esau abandoned the course of violence that he had planned for twenty years. The two brothers embraced, as brothers should.

Jacob's growth and development make him worthy to bear the name Israel. In his transformation, he becomes a worthy role model for us. The Hebrew Bible knows no perfect people. All of its characters have significant flaws. Jacob grows through the mistakes of his youth and becomes the responsible leader of our people. He blesses Joseph's sons and brings them into the Covenant of Abraham. Although he lives as a pensioner in Egypt for seventeen years, he makes his son Joseph swear that he will ensure his burial not in a foreign country but in the land God promised to his fathers, Abraham and Isaac, the land that Abraham purchased at an exorbitant price in the sight of all the people of Heth long ago.

Stephen Lewis Fuchs

CHAPTER VIII

Joseph: A Model for Change

Like Jacob, Joseph acted in an unsavory manner in his youth. Thus, his brothers hated him for four very good reasons (Genesis 37):

1. He was his father's favorite.

2. He was a tattletale.

3. He had grandiose dreams about his superiority, about which he taunted his brothers.

4. He, alone, received the fabled coat of many colors from his father.

When the opportunity presents itself, Joseph's brothers throw him into a pit and then sell him as a slave to Egypt. As a slave, Joseph rises to a position of great responsibility in the home of his master, Potiphar. If the story ended there, we would admire Joseph's remarkable success. That is, however, just the beginning of the tale.

Potiphar's wife tries to seduce Joseph. He resists, claiming that to lie with her would betray his master who had given him so much. Moreover, it would also be "a sin against God" (Genesis 39:9). For Joseph to deflect the advances of the temptress out of regard for his master was completely understandable in the ancient pagan world. One does not mess with the master's wife.

Joseph and the Torah break new moral ground, though, by claiming that to lie with her would also be a sin against God. That notion was unheard of in the pagan world because ancient pagan gods were not concerned with moral behavior. (For this, and many observations regarding the Joseph story, I recognize with gratitude my studies with the great Israeli teacher, Nehama Leibowitz, of blessed memory, at the Hebrew University in Jerusalem in 1970-1971.)

When Joseph resists the advances of Potiphar's wife, she cries rape. With that, Potiphar sentences Joseph to the dungeon. Some commentators plausibly note that Potiphar doubted his wife's claim. For if he believed it, he would have sentenced Joseph to death.

In the dungeon, just as he had in his own home and in Potiphar's house, Joseph rose to a position of superiority. He accurately interpreted the dreams of his cellmates, Pharaoh's cupbearer and baker.

When Pharaoh later experienced dreams that neither he nor his resident experts could interpret, the cupbearer remembered Joseph and mentioned him to Pharaoh. Guards whisked Joseph from the dungeon. They gave him a shave, a haircut, and appropriate clothes—a great literary touch—for what appears will be a brief audience with the most powerful man in the world.

When Pharaoh tells Joseph his dream, we can already see that Joseph has transformed. As a youth, he arrogantly interpreted his own dreams for his brothers. Now, he has the humility to respond to Pharaoh by saying, "It is not I, but God, who will interpret Pharaoh's dreams" (Genesis 41:16). Joseph, like his father before him, learned humility through experience.

Joseph not only interpreted Pharaoh's dream, but also had the *chutzpah* (the nerve)—in what surely must rank as one of the great *carpe diem* moments ever—to give Pharaoh leadership advice as to what to do. Joseph told Pharaoh that Egypt would experience seven years of plenty followed by seven years of severe famine. Joseph offered a conservation plan for the years of plenty and a distribution plan for the years of famine. Pharaoh loved Joseph's plan, and—in a strikingly meteoric rise—Joseph becomes a "star." In an instant, he goes from jailbird to second-in-command in all of Egypt with an Air-Force-Two-like chariot at his disposal.

The seven years of plenty pass quickly. Joseph married and had two sons. The years of famine ensued. Joseph has efficiently stored food during the years of abundance. When the famine began, the entire Mediterranean world came to Egypt to buy food (Genesis 41:46-57). Among the buyers were Joseph's brothers. He recognizes them, but they have no idea that the Egyptian prince who has summoned them to his palace is the brother they sold as a slave twenty years before (Genesis 42).

Jacob sent all of his sons to buy food except Benjamin, his youngest, and the only remaining son of Jacob's beloved wife, Rachel, who died giving birth to him. Benjamin has taken Joseph's place as the apple of his father's eye. Jacob is loath to allow Benjamin to leave home.

Joseph then "goes to work" on his brothers, but not for the reasons described by many commentators. Some claim Joseph put his brothers through their paces for revenge. Some say he wanted his youthful dreams of his brothers humbling themselves before him to come true. Respectfully, I believe these interpretations miss the point.

When he first saw them, Joseph immediately accused his brothers of being spies. He questioned them, and when they revealed they had a younger brother at home, he declared they could never return to buy more food unless that younger brother is with them. He also held one of his brothers, Simeon, hostage. To further disconcert the brothers, he surreptitiously instructed his steward to place the money they brought to purchase food back in their sacks.

When the brothers returned home and told Jacob what happened, he is dismayed and vows that Benjamin will not go to Egypt. He could not stand the thought of losing Benjamin, Rachel's only other child, as well as Joseph.

Nevertheless, three words in Hebrew (eight in English) change his mind: *V'ha-rah-av kah-vade bah-ah-retz,* or "But the famine in the land was severe!" (Genesis 43:1). Finally, Judah confronted his father and (essentially) said, "Either we take the boy and buy food, or we starve. We could have been there and back twice already if we had not dawdled." Judah then swore to his father that he would take full responsibility for the boy's safety, promising, "If I do not bring him back to you, I shall stand guilty before my father forever" (Genesis 43:9).

Reluctantly, Jacob sent Benjamin to Egypt with his brothers. When he saw Benjamin, Joseph immediately afforded him special treatment (as Jacob treated Joseph). He returns Simeon to his brothers and fills all the sacks with food. As the brothers prepared to leave, though, Joseph instructed his chief steward to hide his special goblet in Benjamin's sack, making it look like the boy had stolen it.

After the brothers began their journey home, Joseph sent his officer to apprehend the thief. All of the brothers returned to Egypt after the officer discovered the goblet in Benjamin's sack. Joseph declared that Benjamin must remain in Egypt as his slave.

It is at this point that Judah stepped forward to deliver what is not only the longest single speech in the Bible, but one of the most moving in all of literature. Sir Walter Scott termed Judah's speech, "the most complete pattern of genuine natural eloquence extant in any language" (Joseph Hertz, *Torah Commentary*, p. 169). Judah carefully explained what had happened both on their last visit to Egypt and back home between visits. He then revealed that he pledged himself as surety for Benjamin's safe return to his father. He offers to remain himself as Joseph's slave because, as he relates, if Benjamin does not return home, their father will die. At this moment, Joseph reveals himself to his brothers and forgives them (Genesis 44:18ff.).

The vital question one must ask is why Joseph did this to his brothers. Was it revenge, or was it the realization of his dreams? Both hypotheses lead us astray.

If Joseph wanted revenge, he could have gained it swiftly and decisively. There was no reason to engage his brothers and father in such an elaborate ruse. The moment the brothers appeared before him in Egypt and bowed low to the ground, his boyhood dreams had become manifest. No, Joseph had interest in neither revenge nor dream fulfillment.

Joseph did what he did for only one reason: He needed to know whether his brothers regretted selling him as a slave. After Judah's speech, Joseph knew that Judah, who once suggested selling Joseph away, had matured. Judah and his brothers now realized the pain they had caused their father. When Joseph heard that Judah would even sacrifice his own freedom to safeguard his father from such suffering a second time, Joseph revealed himself to his brothers.

In my studies in Jerusalem with Nehama Leibowitz, I learned that in Jewish thought, a person who commits a sin and repents is as a *ba'al teshuvah*, or a "master of repentance." However, there is another category called *ba'al teshuvah shelema*, or a "master of complete repentance," which aptly describes Judah's action. He had sinned. Then he found himself in the position to commit the same sin again. No one could have blamed Judah had he left Benjamin behind. Surely, it was not his fault that Joseph's goblet appeared in Benjamin's sack. But the same Judah who had sold Joseph would not go home without Benjamin.

From an etiological perspective (the science of causation), Judah's heroism explains why today we are called Jews (after Judah) and not Gadites or Asherites or after any of the other sons of Israel.

From a spiritual perspective, the Joseph story teaches how we can change through repentance. As mentioned earlier, none of Genesis' (or for that matter, the Bible's) characters are plaster saints. They are flesh and blood human beings who "mess up"—often big-time—and grow through those experiences and become better people. Judah is a prime example of this, as are Jacob and Joseph. What worthy and realistic role models they are for all of us as we regret and—when possible—redress the mistakes we all make in our lives.

What transformed Judah? It is important to note the chief biblical catalyst for Judah's metamorphosis was his daughter-in-law, Tamar. Tamar was the wife of Judah's late, eldest son, Er. According to the custom of levirate marriage (a childless widow would marry her husband's brother and bear a child in his name), Tamar married Er's brother, Onan. When he also died, Judah feared the same fate would befall his third son, Shelah. In a misguided effort to save his son's life, Judah broke his promise and did not give Tamar to Shelah in marriage. Instead, Judah sent Tamar to live as a widow in her father's home.

Sometime later, after Judah's own wife dies, and Tamar realized that Judah has allowed her to languish in widowhood; Tamar acted with great courage and resolve. She disguised herself as a prostitute and tempted Judah to have relations with her. As a result, she became pregnant.

When he learned that Tamar was pregnant, Judah was incensed. Yet, when she showed him proof that Judah himself had impregnated her, he was forced to admit, "She is more righteous than I, inasmuch as I did not give her to my son Shelah" (Genesis 38:26).

Although she does not gain a full measure of justice, Tamar refused to be a passive victim of the system, as it then existed. She showed fortitude and courage. She was willing to risk the consequences in order to stand against injustice. Sharon Pace Jeansonne wrote: "Dissatisfaction can either paralyze people or encourage them to fight for what is rightfully theirs. Tamar, fueled by her own resolve to struggle for what she believed in, never gave up" [Sharon Pace Jeansonne, *The Women of Genesis: From Sarah to Potiphar's Wife* (Minneapolis, Augsburg Fortress, 1990), 106].

Tamar's courage not only earned her the offspring she craved, but it also transformed Judah from villain to a hero so worthy that our people bear his name.

After the stunning climax of Joseph revealing himself to his brothers and forgiving them, there is a final scene in Genesis that we must examine. When Joseph forgives his brothers for selling him as a slave, he does so unconditionally. He speaks tenderly to them and sustains them as they make a new life for themselves in the land of Egypt.

Seventeen years later, when Jacob died, the brothers were terrified and exclaimed, "What if Joseph now (that Dad is dead) takes revenge on us and pays us back for all the wrong that we did him?" (Genesis 50:15). On the contrary, Joseph was never interested in revenge. Neither is he now. In one of the most amazing reflections on human destiny, Joseph responded to his terrified siblings, "Have no fear! Am I a substitute for God? Although you intended me harm, God intended it for good, to bring about... the survival of many people...Thus, he reassured them, speaking kindly to them" (Genesis 50:19, 21).

Joseph's tender response to his brothers epitomizes the Jewish outlook on forgiveness. When others seek our pardon for wrongs they have done, we should offer forgiveness graciously, sincerely, and freely as Joseph did to his brothers.

This is the essential message that closes the story of Joseph and the Book of Genesis. Joseph did not blame his brothers because he realized that it was his destiny to come to Egypt to use his talents to save the country from famine.

Each of us has a destiny that we can choose to fulfill. Destiny is different from fate. Fate is inevitable. Destiny is not. We must decide what our destiny is and then make the choice to pursue it. There may be circumstances in our lives that cause us difficulties. Like Joseph, we can look for the opportunity to do good in our times of hardship, or we can simply blame "conditions" or others for our misfortunes. Joseph's response to his brothers, "Although you intended me harm, God intended it for good" (Genesis 50:20), commends itself to us. How we deal with adversity is one of the most important barometers of whether we enhance or diminish the divine image in which God created us.

CHAPTER IX

Slavery: Sensitized to Suffering

Genesis ends with everything neatly wrapped up. The Children of Israel are so comfortable and at-home that Genesis might well have ended with the words "And they all lived happily ever after." The happiness, however, was short-lived. After a quick genealogical summary, the Book of Exodus begins with "There arose a new king who knew not Joseph" (Exodus 1:8). For this new Pharaoh, the Jews quickly became *personae non grata*. He oppressed us, enslaved us, and made our lives miserable.

In the switch from the comfort that marked "Jewish" life at the end of Genesis and the persecution and oppression that quickly overtook us at the outset of Exodus, we have the pattern for Jewish existence in almost every area of the world in which we have ever lived (except North America). When the economy is good, Jews have been welcome and have fared well. When the economy sours, Jews have experienced persecution, expulsion, and extermination. In the United States, for example, anti-Semitism reached its height during the Great Depression.

The reason Passover, celebrating the Exodus from Egypt, has become the most observed Jewish festival is because its events relate directly to what Jews faced in many different societies during the course of history.

The opening chapter of Exodus teaches that there is no guarantee that Jews will always be welcome and free—even in the United States. There is, of course, good reason to hope the freedom of religious expression that the U.S. Constitution guarantees will always protect Jews and other minority faiths. Nevertheless, it would be foolhardy to imagine that the pattern of disillusionment, persecution, and/or expulsion, which has been the Jews' fate in almost every country where we have settled, could not repeat itself here.

CHAPTER X

Six Women Heroes: Where Would We Be without Them?

Contrary to what many claim, women frequently play heroic roles in the Bible. Many are savvier than their husbands. Eve, Rebecca, Tamar, Hannah, Ruth, Vashti, Esther, Samson's (unnamed) mother, and Deborah, are just a few examples of courageous women who changed history and biblical thought. In the story of the Exodus from Egypt, six female heroes play indispensable roles in the unfolding of the story.

Pharaoh's decision regarding the Hebrews to "deal wisely with them" (Exodus 1:10) led to his gruesome instructions to the Hebrew midwives Shiphrah and Puah: "Look at the birth stool: If it is a boy, kill him; If it is a girl, let her live" (Exodus 1:16). The Torah records that Shiphrah and Puah (two of our greatest and most underrated feminine heroes), did not follow Pharaoh's orders. Instead, they saved the baby boys. When Pharaoh called them on the carpet and demanded to know why they ignored his instructions, they replied, "The Hebrew women are just like animals. Before we can get there to assist them, they have already given birth" (Exodus 1:19). The Torah records that the midwives' actions pleased God, who rewarded them for their righteousness (Exodus 1:21).

The examples of Shiphrah and Puah stand as a sharp rebuke for those who excuse their ethical misdeeds with the claim they had no choice—they were simply following orders from their superiors. Case in point: During the trial of Nazi war criminals at Nuremberg, Germany, defendant after defendant attempted to justify his actions on the basis that he was just following orders.[1]

The courage of Shiphrah and Puah is timeless testimony that "just following orders" is no excuse. Each person, every one of us, is personally accountable for all of our actions.

Shiphrah and Puah were not the only female heroes of the Exodus. Except for Moses and his brother Aaron, all of the heroic characters of the Exodus story were women.

Yocheved, Moses' mother, hid her baby in defiance of Pharaoh's decree that all Hebrew baby boys be drowned in the Nile. She placed him in a wicker basket and floated him among the reeds of the Nile. (Exodus 2:2-3).[2]

---

1 Nora Levin, *The Holocaust* (New York: Thomas Y. Crowell Company, 1968), 241-244.

Levin writes that the trial of the commander of Einsatzgruppe D, Otto Ohlendorf, was typical of the Nuremburg proceedings. The American prosecutor Whitney R. Harris asked Ohlendorf, "During the year you were Chief of Einsatzgruppe D, how many men, women, and children did your group kill?"

Ohlendorf shrugged his shoulders and, with only the slightest hesitation, replied, "Ninety thousand."

On the stand later, Judge I. T. Nikitchenko asked, "For what reason were the children massacred?"

"The order," Ohlendorf said evenly, "was that the Jewish population should be totally exterminated..."

When the prosecutor tried to fathom the massacre of children, Ohlendorf was imperturbable. "According to the orders, they were to be killed just like their parents" (p. 242).

2 Interestingly, the word used for the basket in which Moses' floated in the Nile is *tay-vah*, the same word used to describe Noah's ark. These are the only two stories in the Bible where the word is used. Its definition based on its usage is "a waterproof vessel designed to save life." Moses *tay-vah* was the smallest such vessel imaginable. Noah's was the largest.

Stephen Lewis Fuchs

Miriam, Moses' sister, also plays a valiant role in the story. The Bible tells us she watched the basket from afar. Then, when Pharaoh's daughter drew it out of the water, Miriam runs to her and suggests the baby's own mother as its nurse (Exodus 2:6-9).

Rabbinic tradition makes an even greater hero of Miriam than does the Bible.

According to the Talmud, Amram, Moses' father, was the leader of the Hebrews at that time. In order to avoid the pain of Pharaoh's cruel decree that every Hebrew baby boy must drown, Amram ordered all the Hebrew men to divorce their wives. He intended that the Hebrews would not produce any more babies for Pharaoh to kill.

Miriam, however, challenged the wisdom of her father's ruling, saying,

> Father, your decree is more severe than Pharaoh's; because Pharaoh decreed only against the males whereas you have decreed against the males and females...in the case of the wicked Pharaoh, there is a doubt whether his decree will be fulfilled or not, whereas in your case, though you are righteous, it is certain that your decree will be fulfilled. (B. Sotah 12 A)

In effect, Miriam tells her father that he simply cannot give in, nor can he allow the people to give in to Egyptian oppression. In response to Miriam's counsel, Amram remarries his wife, and all the Hebrew men follow suit. Thomas Jefferson eloquently rephrased Miriam's Midrashic advice when he wrote, "Rebellion to tyrants is obedience to God."[3]

---

3   According to *Bartlett's Familiar Quotations* (Boston: Little, Brown and Company, 1955, 1,002B), Jefferson had this quotation inscribed on his personal seal (ca. 1776).

Pharaoh's daughter plays a heroic role in the story by saving Moses and raising him as her son (Exodus 2:11-12). The Talmud emphasizes that Pharaoh's daughter was apprised of the gravity of her action:

> When her maidens saw that she wished to rescue Moses, they said to her, Mistress, it is the custom of the world that when a human king makes a decree, though everybody else does not obey it, at least his children and the members of his household obey it; but you are transgressing your father's decree. (B. Sotah 12B)

Still, Pharaoh's daughter defies her father, her King, and her god-Pharaoh and saves Moses. For this, she receives the privilege of giving Moses his name; and she herself was given the name *Bityah,* which means, "Daughter of the Lord" (B. Sotah 12B).

The other female hero of the Exodus story is Zipporah, Moses' wife. When Moses is returning from exile in Midian to confront Pharaoh and demand the release of the Hebrew slaves, an obscure passage, seemingly unrelated to what comes before and after, intrudes into the biblical text:

> At a night encampment on the way, the Lord met him and sought to kill him. So Zipporah took a flint and cut off her son's foreskin and touched his legs with it saying, "You are truly a bridegroom of blood to me." And when He (God) let him alone, she added, "A bridegroom of blood because of the circumcision." (Exodus 4:24-26)

This passage is confusing because it does not connect to the passages that come before and after. The rabbis could interpret it to mean almost anything they chose. It is significant that they chose to interpret it to say that Zipporah's quick thinking and bold action in circumcising her son actually saved Moses' life. They wrote, "So beloved is circumcision that Moses' punishment for its neglect was not suspended even for one hour." Zipporah realized Moses' life was in jeopardy and saved it by circumcising their son, Eleazar (Shemot Rabbah 5:8).

The rabbis' deliberate efforts to embellish the role of women in stories surrounding the Jews' most popular religious celebration are often overlooked by those who contend that women suffered low status in traditional Judaism. It is unfair to compare the cultural standards of religious tradition, which are more than 2,000 years old, with our expectations and standards today. Compared with other cultures in the Talmudic era (200 BCE-500 CE), Jewish women enjoyed many advantages. Clearly, the rabbis worked diligently to upgrade the status of women in the Talmudic period compared with their status as biblical legislation and custom portray it. Just as clearly, women in the Bible often play heroic roles.

Although Moses is the main character in the Exodus narrative and indeed the main character in the entire Torah, Moses never would have said, "Let my people go!" to Pharaoh were it not for these six women. Throughout our journey from the Creation to the edge of the Promised Land, and throughout the Bible as well, we see that women play vital strong roles in the Bible, while their male counterparts often stand by, clueless.

Stephen Lewis Fuchs

CHAPTER XI

Moses: He Answered the Call to Conscience. Will We?

Moses grows up as an Egyptian prince. According to the Midrash, his mother, Yocheved, teaches him about his heritage and the importance of loyalty to his people. Her efforts pay off. One day, as Moses walks among the Hebrew slaves he encounters an Egyptian taskmaster beating one of them. An Egyptian prince should not care, but Moses smites the Egyptian.

In one of the most profound of all Midrashic statements, the Eternal One observes Moses' action and says, "Moses, if you have descended from your high station to take up the case of a Hebrew slave, then it is time for Me to descend from my high station and redeem my people, the Children of Israel" (Shemot Rabbah 2:2).

Wow. It doesn't get more dramatic than that. Imagine, through our acts of righteousness, we are capable of influencing the Almighty. The notion of a God responding positively to human goodness is one of the most revolutionary ideas in the Torah.

Unfortunately, because he smote the taskmaster, Moses has to leave Egypt and his princely status behind. Again, he is a role model for us and encourages us to consider one of life's most vital questions: What is more important? Success and reward? Or doing what is just and right?

Moses traverses the desert, arrives in Midian, meets (like Jacob and Isaac) his wife-to-be at a well, and eventually settles into a comfortable existence as shepherd for his father-in-law, the Midianite priest, Jethro.

Later, Moses encounters God, calling him back to Egypt from a burning bush. A burning bush, as the rabbis note, was hardly a dramatic event in the desert. It took a person with extraordinary insight to realize the bush did not go up in flames, and to listen to the voice of God calling from within [Louis Ginzberg, *Legends of the Jews*, (Philadelphia, Jewish Publication Society of America, 1968) Vol. 2, 304].

People often ask me, "Why doesn't God speak with us anymore?" I believe God does, but we must learn how to listen to God's voice. Like Cain, we can choose to ignore the voice or defy it. If we train ourselves to not only hear, but to listen, God will speak to us in the voice of our conscience—just as God spoke long ago. We must strive to recognize that voice urging us to choose the path of righteousness and justice over that of expedience and narrow self-interest.

Although Moses clearly heard God's voice, initially, he was reluctant to heed it. He throws every possible excuse at the Almighty: "Who am I," he asks, "to go before Pharaoh? I don't speak very well." But God would not be dissuaded (Exodus 3 and 4).

The task God had chosen Moses to undertake was enormous. Moses had to convince himself, that he was the man for the job. Fortunately, Moses heeded God's voice and fulfilled his destiny.

Perhaps there is only one real difference between Moses and Cain. Cain turned away from God's call, but Moses obeyed it.

Think of it. The Torah teaches that our lives *can* have purpose and meaning. The rest is up to us. God wants us to try our best—setbacks and frustrations notwithstanding—to use our talents to make the world better. We do not all have the ability to lead a nation, cure cancer, or invent a life-changing device, but we all can do something to make life better for others. Cain said no to God. Moses said yes. Perhaps the most important question we can ask ourselves is, "What will our answer be when God—in whatever mysterious way God chooses—affords us a glimpse of our potential destiny?"

Stephen Lewis Fuchs

CHAPTER XII

God's Role in the Exodus

When Moses finally makes the long trek back to Egypt, he hears God say something very puzzling: "I have hardened Pharaoh's heart so that he will not listen to you." In other words, God warns Moses, "This is not going to be easy."

I vividly remember the first Introduction to Judaism class I taught as a young rabbi. When we discussed the Exodus, a woman raised her hand and challenged me with this question: "What kind of an evil God would harden Pharaoh's heart? If God is so powerful, why did He not simply soften Pharaoh's heart so that he would give up the slaves willingly?"

It certainly would have been lovely if when Moses came to Pharaoh and said, "Let my people go!" Pharaoh would have said, "Certainly, Moses. You know, as I think about it, it was not very nice of me to enslave your people and treat them so harshly."

"Of course, I shall let them go."

Yes, it would indeed be wonderful if the world worked that way. Here again, though, the Torah is telling us more about the way the world is than the way it should be. In the real world, tyrants—from Pharaoh to Hitler to the guardians of apartheid in South Africa and the segregation of races in the United States—do not give up their power without a colossal struggle.

To understand the Exodus narrative, we must view it as a war—a boxing match if you will—between gods. In one corner, we have the Egyptian god, Pharaoh. Pharaoh is like any pagan god. One worships him by glorifying him with monuments, pyramids, sphinxes, and garrison cities. If slaves are required in order to build these structures, so be it. If it is necessary to beat those slaves in order to keep them working, or even kill one or two occasionally to send a message, that is fine too. And if over-population becomes an issue (see the First Chapter of Exodus), simply throw their baby boys into the Nile.

In the other corner, though, we have the one true God of the Hebrew Bible, who created us in God's image. God's highest goal is that we create a just, caring, and compassionate society. God wants us to treat one another with respect and dignity. God wants us not to steal, cheat, or lie. God has particular concern for the powerless of society; the widow, the orphan, the outsider, the abused, and the impoverished. The contrasting value systems represented by Pharaoh and God cannot coexist peacefully.

Imagine the scene from many a Western movie in which the sheriff says to the bad guy, "This town ain't big enough for both of us," and a showdown ensues. Well, Exodus is a showdown between God and Pharaoh. Because it is our story, our God wins by redeeming us from slavery and bringing us to Mount Sinai, where God renews and expands with an entire people, the sacred covenant God once made with just Abraham and his family.

Because God intervenes in history so dramatically, we owe God a debt we can never fully repay. Imagine for a moment that you are watching your small toddler. Something distracts you, and in a split second, your child has wandered into the middle of the street. You look up, see a large truck bearing down on him, and realize with terror that there is no way you can save him. In the nick of time a woman dashes into the street, grabs the child, and pulls him to safety. There is no way, of course, that you can adequately repay that woman for saving your child.

In the same way God saved us. Our lives were hopeless. We lived in drudgery and oppression. We never knew when we might be beaten or killed. Life had neither meaning nor purpose. Suddenly, God delivered us. Because of that, we freely choose how we will earn a living, how we will spend our leisure, and how or if we will worship. In short, we believe we owe God a debt that we can never repay.

Yet, we try. We try by performing acts of kindness, caring, and compassion. We attempt to establish justice and righteousness in society.

Yes, it would be lovely if God simply softened Pharaoh's heart, but life does not work that way. Moreover, the vital lessons of the Exodus story and the moral imperatives they impose upon us would not find such clear, dramatic, and instructive illustration.

Hardening Pharaoh's heart does not mean that God literally makes Pharaoh act in an evil way. It means that Pharaoh, like all of us, has free will. From a psychological viewpoint, the more one turns away from the voice of conscience (which I consider to be the voice of God), the easier it is to resist that voice.

In *Studies in Shemot*, Nehama Leibowitz compares the unchecked acts that evil Pharaoh committed, to those of Macbeth. At first, Macbeth is reluctant to do wrong. He certainly fears laying hands on his king, Duncan. With each succeeding murder, though, the voice of his conscience exercises less and less control over his treacherous impulses.

When in Act III, Lady Macbeth, who first encouraged her reluctant husband to kill the king, voices her reservations about

Macbeth's ruthless reign of terror, Macbeth responds, "Things bad begun make strong themselves by ill" (Act III, Scene 2, Line 55). In other words, the evil has taken on a life of its own. Macbeth can no longer control himself. So it was with Pharaoh.

In rabbinic literature, belief in God and the study of the Torah align to help us fight the inclination to do evil. Rabbi Simeon ben Levi said, "The evil inclination of a person waxes stronger day by day. It seeks to kill him. If God does not help, a person could not overcome it" (B. Kiddushin 30 b).

Implicit in this text is the notion that a person must enlist God's help to fight the inclination to do evil. God will not do it for us unless we consciously make the effort. Rabbi Akiva (second century CE) foreshadowed Shakespeare's insight in Macbeth when he described the inclination to do evil this way: "At first it (the inclination to do evil) is like a spider's thread and at last it is like a rope of a ship" (Genesis Rabbah 22:6).

In other words, when we persist in evil or when we ignore God's will, evil takes on strength greater than we can control.

God, then, did not actually harden Pharaoh's heart. God allowed Pharaoh to continue on the course that he had chosen. God allows all of us to do the same. Although most of us, at one time or another, have wished that God would step in and change people, such action would rob us all, of the free will, that gives life meaning.

With regard to the Exodus, people often ask, "Why did God free us from Egypt, but not from the Holocaust?" Actually, the two events are more similar than different. In neither did God stop the tyranny immediately. We were slaves in Egypt for 430 years according to the biblical text (Exodus 12:40). By contrast, The Holocaust lasted twelve years.

There is a vigorous scholarly debate today over whether the events described in Exodus actually happened. There is no mention in Egyptian sources of Hebrew slaves or anything else to corroborate the Exodus account. I am more than willing to leave this debate to those who spend their lives researching such questions.

For me, whether the events described in the Bible actually took place is not a crucial question. Of vital interest to me is what the story teaches. The Exodus story teaches me that in exchange for all that God has done for me, I want to spend my life trying to live up to God's hopes and ideals. All too often, I fall short. There is much about God that remains a mystery. However, despite the many unanswered questions, the text inspires me to believe that God wants all of us to use our talents to make the world a better place.

Stephen Lewis Fuchs

CHAPTER XIII

Crossing the Sea: Balance Due

In Exodus 14:10-14, the Children of Israel see the Egyptians bearing down on them as they stand at the banks of the Sea of Reeds. The people panic and blame Moses for their plight, saying, "Was it for want of graves in Egypt that you brought us to die in the wilderness? What have you done to us taking us out of Egypt?" (Exodus 14:11-12).

Moses responds that the people should have no fear. God will protect them (Exodus 14:13-14).

At this point, God speaks to Moses, saying, "Why do you cry out to Me? Tell the Israelites to go forward" (Exodus 14:15). The rabbis interpret Moses' response to the Children of Israel as a prayer to which God responded that there is a time for prayer and a time for action. This was the time for action. In the words of the Midrash,

> God said to Moses: "There is at time to shorten prayers, there is a time to draw them out. My children are in dire distress, The sea has fenced them in, and the enemy is pursuing. So, how can you stand there and multiply prayers?! Tell the children of Israel to go forward." (Exodus 14:15) (Shemot Rabbah 21:8)

In rabbinic literature, there are conflicting traditions as to how the Israelites respond to Moses' command to go forward. The rabbis never perceived a need to resolve these conflicting views. They taught that a text can have many meanings and teach many lessons.

One interpretation is that everyone argued about who would have the honor of going in the water first. After much contention, the tribe of Benjamin succeeded in entering the water before the other tribes; according to this tradition, God rewarded them by having the temple built in their territory (B. Sotah 36B-37A). The story also explains why a member of the tribe of Benjamin, Saul, was chosen to be the first king of Israel.

A more familiar and contradictory tradition is another etiological account written to explain why the tribe of Judah became the dominant tribe and the only one that ultimately survived. It helps us understand, once again, why we have taken the name Jews. The text reads,

> Each tribe was unwilling to be the first to enter the sea. Then sprang forward Nachshon ben Amminadab (chieftain of the tribe of Judah) and descended first into the sea. (B. Sotah 37A)

A third view, and my favorite interpretation, contends that God did not part the waters until the Israelites as a group showed their faith in God's power. The Midrash states that the sea was divided only after Israel had stepped into it and the waters had reached their noses. Only then did it become dry land (Shemot Rabbah 21:10).

Here, the rabbis teach us all an important religious lesson. The deliverance from Egypt was not accomplished *only* because of God's will and God's miracles. Our salvation was a covenantal partnership requiring not only God's power, but Israel's faith as well. From a biblical perspective, God simply parted the sea. From the rabbinic perspective of this Midrash, however, the Israelites as a group demonstrated their worthiness for redemption by wading into the water up to their noses before the sea parted.

Jewish tradition does not question the validity of God's actions in drowning the Egyptian pursuers. Still, while we rejoice in our freedom, we take no delight in the destruction of our enemy. The Talmud states,

> When the Egyptian armies were drowning in the sea, the ministering angels broke out in songs of jubilation. God silenced them, saying, "The works of My hands are drowning in the sea. How can you sing praises in My presence?!" (B. Sanhedrin 39B)

At the Seder meal that celebrates Passover, participants traditionally remove a drop of wine from their cups as each of the ten plagues against Egypt is recited. Wine is a symbol of joy in Jewish practice. By taking wine out of our cups, we diminish our joy in recognition of the suffering of our enemies.

An important figure in modern Jewish history expressed a similar sentiment. Israel's troops were not fully prepared for the Egyptian invasion, which was launched on Yom Kippur in 1973. Even though Israel managed to thwart the military challenge, there was no rejoicing in the Jewish state. There was instead a lingering feeling of sadness because of all the casualties suffered on both sides. In the aftermath of Israel's victory, Prime Minister Golda Meir spoke in a manner reminiscent of the Talmudic passage above when she said, "You know, the Arabs' greatest sin is not making war against Israel and killing her sons. We can forgive them for that. Their greatest sin is that they made us kill them" [Margaret Davidson, *The Golda Meir Story*, rev. ed. (New York, Charles Scribner's Sons, 1981, p. 206)].

Stephen Lewis Fuchs

CHAPTER XIV

A Visit from Jethro: Management 101

After crossing the Sea of Reeds, we eventually arrive at Sinai, and Moses' father-in-law, Jethro, pays the Israelites a visit. (I use the term "we" intentionally. Midrashic tradition holds that all the unborn generations of the Jewish people were somehow present as the Children of Israel stood at Mount Sinai to receive the Torah.) When Jethro sees how Moses occupies himself in judging the disputes of the people from early morning until late at night, he takes him aside and says in effect, "Moses, at this rate, you will burn out very quickly. You are trying to do much too much. You need to learn how to delegate. Set up divisions among the people and create a structure of increasing authority. Let only the most important matters come to you personally. If you do this, you will be able to successfully lead the people on their journey" (Exodus 18).

Jethro could easily say those words to so many of us today. With our technologically advanced world, we are attached to our work—unless we choose otherwise—twenty-four hours a day, seven days a week. We multi-task, we run from place-to-place and from meeting-to-meeting. We suffer the risk of burnout just as Moses would have without Jethro's advice more than three thousand years ago.

Jethro's visit reminds us how relevant biblical teaching is to our contemporary world. All of us who find ourselves trying to do too much in too little time should heed his advice. We must prioritize and delegate responsibility. In so doing, we become better employers, employees, husbands, wives, mothers, fathers, and creatures created in God's image. We should remember that we are here to use our talents not just to pile up lists of accomplishments, but to make this world a better place.

CHAPTER XV

Standing at Sinai: Highest of Highs

Finally, the moment toward which the entire Torah aims arrives: the revelation of the Torah on Mount Sinai. So unique in history did our sages envision the event at Sinai. They imagined the world coming to a silent standstill. In the words of the Midrash,

> When God gave the Torah, no bird twittered, no fowl flew, no ox grunted...the sea did not roar, the whole world hushed in breathless silence, and the Divine voice went forth proclaiming (Exodus 20:2): "I am the Lord your God; who brought you out of the land of Egypt, out of the house of bondage." (Shemot Rabbah 29:9)

What makes this moment so unique? For all subsequent generations of Jews, the moment of the revelation of the Torah at Mount Sinai symbolizes our acceptance of our covenantal obligations. Now, the covenant God made first with Abraham, alone, becomes the privilege and sacred responsibility of all Jewish people—past, present, and future.

It should surprise no one that our sages' fertile minds produced a number of thought-provoking Midrashim. Each is instructive.

In one Midrash, God offers the Torah to all the nations of the world. But when they hear what it says (e.g., "Don't cheat," "Don't steal," "Treat the stranger, the widow, the orphan, and the poor with special dignity and respect"), they quickly reject it (Sefer Ha-Agadah, Bialik and Rovenitzky, eds., vol. 1, p. 59).

Another Midrash I like to call *The Godfather* Midrash, God makes an offer the Children of Israel cannot refuse. God lifts Mount Sinai and holds it over the heads of the assembled children of Israel. Then God says, "Either you accept and pledge to observe my Torah, or I shall drop the mountain on top of you" (B. Shabbat 88A and B. Avodah Zarah 2B).

This Midrash teaches us the vital lesson that our only purpose as a people is to be teachers and examples of the ideals of the Torah to the world. Indeed, by adherence to these ideals, we become, in the words of the prophet Isaiah, "a light to the nations" (Isaiah 49:6), a worthy example for all. If, however, we are not willing to accept the responsibility of adhering to the Torah's ideals, there is no good reason for us to continue to exist.

The lesson of that Midrash is as true today as when it was written. We do not wish everyone to be Jewish, but we have our distinctive ways that have contributed greatly to enhancing world civilization. It is our sacred obligation to study, learn, teach, and practice the Torah's teachings, then pass those ideals on to future generations.

There is even a Midrash stating that Israel's willingness to accept the Torah was of the utmost importance to God. In fact, the Almighty threatened to break the post-flood promise never again to destroy the world, unless Israel agrees to embrace the Torah and its ideals (B. Shabbat 88A).

The importance of passing on the Torah's teachings finds fuller expression in yet another Midrash. Here, the question is not "Are we willing to accept the Torah?" It is rather, "How will we demonstrate to God that we are worthy to receive it?" When God asks us to offer guarantors of our worthiness, we offer the deeds of the great patriarchs (Abraham, Isaac, and Jacob) and the deeds of the prophets, but God finds neither of these pledges acceptable. Only when we pledge the loyalty of our children to God's teachings does God reveal the Torah to our people (Shir Ha Shirim Rabbah, Chapter 1, Section 4, Midrash 1).

One swiftly perceives that even on such crucial issues as to the occurrences at Sinai, and what was at stake, our sages had conflicting ideas. Here are some:

1. That before offering it to Israel, God offered the Torah to all the nations of the world, but none of them wanted it.

2. That God threatened to destroy Israel if they did not accept it.

3. Moreover, that God would destroy the entire world if we did not accept the Torah.

4. That God would not entrust us with the Torah unless we pledged our children and future generations that we would be loyal to its teachings.

The thinking person is, of course, free to accept any or none of these interpretations. The rabbinic method of interpretation encouraged creative thought. There was rarely only one acceptable point of view on any question. The sages certainly took their Scripture seriously, but they also saw the Bible as in need of interpretation, and there was never a requirement for them to resolve the conflicts that they had.

History has imposed great changes in Jewish life over the millennia. But the place of the Torah at the heart and soul of our religious quest has never changed. The durability of the Torah never proved more important than when the Romans destroyed the second temple in Jerusalem in the year 70 CE.

While it stood, the temple was the physical and emotional heart of the Jewish people. It was literally God's home, run by a hereditary priestly class whom, as our people believed, the Almighty had anointed for that purpose. It was the only place where the priest offered the animal sacrifices—through which they communicated the hopes, dreams, laments, and petitions of the people—to God.

By all logic, Judaism should have disappeared when the Romans destroyed the temple, in 70 CE. With the destruction of the temple the three main pillars of Jewish life (the hereditary priesthood, animal sacrifice, and the Temple in Jerusalem as God's home base) no longer existed.

Fortunately, the Pharisees and their successors saved Judaism by instituting new bases for Jewish life to replace those they had lost. The study of the Torah and its teachings, formal prayer, and acts of kindness and compassion were the new means of showing loyalty to God and faithfulness to our sacred covenant.

Traditional Jews pray regularly for the restoration of the temple. I do not. I much prefer, as do most, a religion based on study, prayer, and acts of kindness to illustrate my solidarity with God's principles.

Stephen Lewis Fuchs

CHAPTER XVI

The Golden Calf: Lowest of Lows

No sooner does Israel declare her allegiance to God and God's covenant than she falls off the wagon. Moses is gone forty days and nights, and during that time the Israelites become frightened. They are still very much in a slave mentality. And without the guidance of a visible leader, they lose it. They turn on Aaron and demand, "Give us a god we can see," because who knows what has become of this Moses.

Aaron, to his discredit, utters not a whimper of protest. He tells the people to bring him their jewelry, and fashions an idol, a golden calf for them to worship.

"Why," I have often been asked, "is Aaron not punished for his complicity in the peoples' apostasy?" From a historical perspective, the answer is simple. It was Aaron and his descendants who had taken control of Israelite life at the time the Torah attained its present form. His descendants give us the Torah as we now have it.

The logical follow-up questions then are: Why is the story recorded at all? If Aaron and his descendants had the power, why put something in the biblical narrative, which reflects so negatively on the first high priest of Israel?

The answer is that the memory of the golden calf incident was much too vivid to extirpate. It would be akin to editing the assassination of President John F. Kennedy from the history books of the United States.

Hence, the priestly redactors of the Torah did the next best thing regarding the golden calf episode. They buried it. They did not place in its logical place after the Ten Commandments and the laws, which followed them. Those who edited the final version of the Book of Exodus hid the golden calf incident in the midst of two long, and to some, boring accounts of the intricate details of the building of the desert tabernacle.

The Torah records: God tells Moses to hurry down from the mount as the Children of Israel have run amok. They have forsaken God's wishes in favor of building an idolatrous calf to worship. God threatens to destroy the entire people, but Moses stays God's hand, and asks, "How will it look to Egypt?" The Egyptians will think that You destroyed the people because you were not powerful enough to deliver them to the Promised Land. Now God might not have been a bit worried about how it would look to Egypt, but the point is that God and Moses were in partnership; and God heeded Moses entreaty to forgive the people's great sin.

Then, Moses himself loses it. When he sees the people reveling before the calf in orgiastic fashion, he becomes so enraged that he hurls the tablets of the Covenant to the ground, smashing them to bits.

Eventually, God calms down, and Moses calms down. When it is time to put the incident behind them, God seems to take Moses to task for smashing the tablets. "Hew out two tablets of stone like the first," God commands (Exodus 34:1).

The implication is that although Moses had a right to be furious, he had no right to smash the tablets. This time, he has to hew them out himself instead of God providing them as (the text seems to suggest) God did the first time. The lesson for us is that we take much better care of something in which we have invested time and energy to create.

The rabbis take the story and its lesson a step forward in this marvelous Midrash. "Rabbi Judah bar Ilai taught: Two Arks journeyed with Israel in the wilderness in which the Torah was placed, and the other in which the Tablets broken by Moses were placed…" (Palestinian Talmud, Shekalim 1:1).

Wow. The Midrash teaches us that we can learn at least as much from our mistakes and failings as we can from our triumphs. We all make mistakes—even big ones. But if we turn our failings into instructive lessons rather than letting them destroy our sense of purpose and self-worth, they can be of enormous benefit.

The golden calf story is a strong warning to all of us not to overvalue material things. One of my favorite prayers is, "Help me, O God, to distinguish between that which is real and enduring and that which is fleeting and vain."

Ray Stevens makes this prayer concrete for us aptly in a popular song of yesteryear:

> "Itemize the things you covet as you squander through
> your life – bigger cars, bigger houses, term insurance
> for your wife!…Did you see your children growing up
> today? Did you hear the music of their laughter as they
> set about to play? Did you catch the fragrance of those
> roses in your garden? Did the morning sunlight warm
> your soul, brighten up your day? Spending counterfeit
> incentive, wasting precious time and health, placing
> value on the worthless disregarding priceless wealth."
> (Ray Stevens, "Mr. Businessman," 1968)

In essence, God brought us out of Egypt not just to be free of Pharaoh's oppression, but also that we would be free to journey to Mount Sinai and accept responsibility for the Covenant God made with Abraham. Accepting responsibility means that we use our talents to create a more just, caring, and compassionate society. It is easy to lose sight of those values in our rush to make a living. During our time off, we rush around with the goal of amassing bigger, better, and shinier material goods.

Indeed, the golden calf is alive and well. It lives in our cities and towns, and if we allow it, the turbo-charged golden calf of today will take over *our* hearts and minds, as well.

The golden calf narrative is a quintessential illustration of the middle ground of biblical understanding. Who knows if there was a golden calf, and whether God became furious at our worshipping it. I do not take the story literally, but the truth of the Bible is not literal truth. On the other hand, I do not simply dismiss it as an ancient fairy tale. The truth of the story is in its message, a message that can change our lives if we take it to heart.

Stephen Lewis Fuchs

CHAPTER XVII

The Spies: Moses Stays God's Hand Again

Moses' restraining God's anger when God threatens to destroy the Children of Israel is repeated in another famous story. In the second year of their journey, God instructs Moses to send twelve scouts, one from each of the twelve Israelite tribes, to spy on the Promised Land (Numbers 13 ff). Moses requests that the spies bring back a detailed report of the land they plan to invade and conquer. The spies return and tell Moses, essentially, there is good news and bad news. The good news is that the land is wonderful. It is rich and fertile; it "flows with milk and honey" (Numbers 13:27). To prove their point, the spies return with a cluster of grapes so rich and lush that it took two men to bear the pole to which the grapes were attached (Numbers 13:23).

The bad news, according to ten of the twelve scouts, is that the land is unconquerable. The people are "giants" and we will seem to them "like grasshoppers" (Numbers 14:33).

Two of the scouts, Joshua and Caleb, disagree contending that God has promised us this land, and we need to have the faith and courage to do our part and carry out God's plan.

Nevertheless, the naysayers were so easy to dissuade. They rail against Moses for 'rescuing' them from Egypt only to die out in the wilderness. "It would be better for us to go back to Egypt. Let us head back for Egypt (Numbers 14:3-4)."

Once again, God is angry enough at the people's lack of faith to destroy them. Once again, Moses stands between the people and God's anger. Using the same argument as with the golden calf, Moses, says: "When the Egyptians, from whose midst You brought up this people in Your might, hear the news, they will tell it to the inhabitants of that land...If then You slay this people to a man the nations who have heard Your fame will say, It must be because the Lord was powerless to bring that people into the land He had promised them on oath that He slaughtered them in the wilderness" (Numbers 14:13-16).

Moses' appeal to God's concern for the divine reputation is an example of biblical humor that misleads some into labeling God as a vain and self-absorbed deity. *Au contraire.* God could not care less what either the Egyptians or other nations think. The intent is to demonstrate the sacred partnership between God and Moses.

Those times when he restrains God's wrath are Moses' finest hours. Even though God promises to glorify Moses with a new and improved nation, Moses will not have it. This is Your people, Moses insists, whom You freed from the land of Egypt. You cannot destroy them. The crucial message of this incident—as with the golden calf—is that Moses and God are partners. When God seemed ready to give up on the people, Moses offered encouragement, perspective and hope. When Moses runs out of faith, God strengthens him.

I hope that it is that way with us. When life is most difficult, with a bit of luck, we hear a voice within—I call it God—that urges us to continue; to believe in ourselves and that our lives have purpose. And, when evil and violence surround us, and it seems that God cannot be found, we must "...be still and know...(Psalm 46:10)." Through our god-like acts of compassion and sharing, we inspire God's compassion just as Moses had done.

Stephen Lewis Fuchs

CHAPTER XVIII

The Waters of Meribah: Was God Unfair?

After nearly forty years of leading the Children of Israel through the wilderness, Moses is near the end of his rope. He snaps when the Israelites complain yet again that they have no water. God tells Moses to address a certain rock, and water will come forth. Instead of addressing the rock, Moses, still in mourning over the death of his sister, Miriam, loses his temper and shouts, "Listen you rebels. Shall we indeed bring forth water from this rock" (Numbers 20:10). And then he bangs his staff three times against the rock as water comes gushing forth.

God is furious! Moses has made it appear that he—not the Almighty had caused the rock to issue water. However, furious or not, God imposes a penalty that seems unduly harsh. "Because you did not show enough faith in me to affirm my holiness in the eyes of the Children of Israel, you shall not lead the community into the land I am giving them" (Numbers 20:12). Wow! After all Moses had done, God sentences him to die in the wilderness without ever entering the Promised Land! How could God be so cruel? It is like giving someone a life sentence for a relatively minor violation. Even if we argue that, the offense was indeed serious (and I would agree) the punishment seems too harsh.

Ultimately, ranting against God's excess misses the point. There is a vital lesson in this story for all of us. Moses' time had passed. He was not the leader he once was. He was too old to lead the military campaign necessary for the Israelites to conquer the Promised Land.

Such a campaign required a young, vigorous leader whose voice the people would obey without hesitation. Joshua was that man, and if Moses were still around when Joshua said, "Charge!" there would be those who would look to Moses to see if "Charge!" was, in fact, the right thing to do.

Each of us has limited opportunities to lead and to influence. When that time passes, even if we are Moses, we have to step aside and pass the reigns of leadership on to another. The question of whether God's punishment was too harsh is irrelevant. Moses was past his prime as all of us will be one day. Therefore, we should make the most of the opportunities afforded us. Too many people lament what they should have done when they had the chance. Time is finite, and so like Moses, we must do what we can, when we can. Unlike Moses, though, we must be ready to relinquish the reigns when that time is over.

Chapter XIX

What If I Don't Believe in God?

At the core of Jewish thought is the assumption that God exists. Without question, the concept of a single good, caring God who wants us to use our talents to make the world a better place is at the base of all Jewish thought and practice. Yet, what about those who don't believe in such a God, or any God at all?

Can Jewish learning be meaningful and beneficial to them? Indeed, it can, without a doubt.

In Noah Gordon's novel *The Rabbi,* young Michael Kind intervenes to rescue Rabbi Max Gross from a New York City mugging. The encounter with the rabbi stimulates in Michael questions about his own beliefs. He returns to the rabbi's apartment and says,

"Tell me about God."

"What is it that you want to know?"

"How can you be sure that man didn't imagine God because he was afraid of the dark and the lousy cold, because he needed the protection of anything, even his own stupid imagination...I think I've become an agnostic."

"No, no, no," Rabbi Gross responded. "Then call yourself an atheist. Because how can anyone be certain that God exists...Do you think I have knowledge of God? Can I go back in time and be there when God speaks to Isaac or delivers the commandments? If this could be done, there would only be one religion in the world. We would all know which group is right. Now it happens to be the way of all men to take sides. A person has to make a decision. About God, you don't know, and I don't know. But I have made a decision in favor of God. You have made a decision against Him."

"I've made no decisions," Michael said a bit sullenly. "That's why I'm here. I'm full of questions. I want to study with you."

Rabbi Gross touched the books piled on his table. "A lot of great thoughts are contained here," he said. "But they don't hold the answer to your question. They can't help you decide. First, you make a decision. Then we will study."

"No matter what I decide? Suppose I think God is a fable, a *bubbeh-meisir*."

"No matter."

Outside in the dark hallway, Michael looked back at the closed door of the shul. "Goddamn you," he thought. And then in spite of everything, he smiled at his choice of words. [Noah Gordon, *The Rabbi* (New York, McGraw-Hill Book Company, 1965), pp. 132-134]

Like young Michael, many of us do not believe in God. Many of us do not believe in a God who judges us.

The Jewish High Holy Days of Rosh Hashanah and Yom Kippur, the Jewish New Year, and the Jewish day of Atonement are ten days apart on the Jewish calendar. The two holy days and the days between them are a time for introspection and contemplation of one's life and actions during the past year, a time for reflection and repentance.

The most stark, and for many, most difficult prayer of the High Holy Day season is the *Unetaneh Tokef*, which we pray at the morning service on the holy days. The words, *Unetaneh Tokef*, mean, "Let us acknowledge the enormity of this sacred day."

On Rosh Hashanah, it is written, and Yom Kippur, it is sealed:

how many shall pass on and how many shall come to be

who shall live and who shall die; who shall see ripe old age and who shall not;

who shall perish by fire and who by water; who by sword and who by beast;

who by hunger and who by thirst.

But repentance, prayer, and charity temper judgment's severe decree.

I certainly do not believe, and no one I know believes, that those who died in the past year died because they were deficient in repentance, prayer, and charity.

None of us knows who shall live and who shall die in the coming year. To a great degree, how long we live is beyond our control, but *how* we live is up to us.

We can unlock the door of unbelief that stands between many of us, and the purpose, and the prayers of this day, with a single Hebrew word, *k'eeloo,* which means "as if."

It is a simple concept. Whatever our beliefs, if we can act *k'eeloo* ("as if") we stand under God's scrutiny, we shall make a giant leap forward.

The word Israel in Hebrew is Yisrael, which means "one who struggles with God." It does not mean "one who believes in God," and it does not mean "one who is always comfortable with God." The High Holy Days invite us to serious struggle and effort.

The *Unetaneh Tokef* prayer is one of the best "struggling tools" ever. It has the power to change our lives.

Once, during the Russo-Japanese War at the beginning of the twentieth century, S. Y. Agnon writes in *Days of Awe*, "A committee of Jewish soldiers passed through all the hospitals and announced there would be public prayer" for the holy days.

"It was an awful sight. Many of those who came were incapacitated, gloomy, and lean as corpses; many...were armless, lame, and blind; leaned on crutches, and bore wounds of every day description...

"During the *Unetaneh Tokef* prayer, no words were heard in the house of prayer; only tear-choked voices filled the atmosphere of the little house. The cantor's voice became stronger, stronger, and struck sparks in the air: 'Who will live and who will die,... Before his time.' Those were terrible and awful moments." [S.Y. Agnon, *The Days of Awe* (New York, Schocken Books, 1965), pp.104-105]

How many of these men were believers? I do not know, but the real possibility of imminent death gave urgency and meaning to their prayers.

The purpose of the Jewish holy day of Yom Kippur is to imagine our imminent death.

On Yom Kippur, Jews separate ourselves from bodily pleasures. We imagine that we have died, and we envision ourselves trembling before the throne of a God who calls us to account for our actions.

Even if we do not believe in God, is it not well for us to try to answer the questions our tradition ascribes to God?

How did we use the time we had?

Did we use our abilities simply to provide for ourselves, or did we work to make the world a better place? What did we do last year that we wish we could change?

Actions in the Jewish religion are more important than beliefs. That is one of the vital differences between Jewish and classical Christian thinking.

The Jerusalem Talmud ascribes the following quotation to God: "Would that My people forsake Me, but keep my commandments!" (Hagigah 1:7).

Elie Wiesel was a young journalist living in Israel when he published his first book, *Night*, in 1958. Once, he had been a budding Talmud scholar, an *ilui*, a gifted one, a genius.

He was, in the words of Francois Mauriac, "one of God's elect. From the time when his conscience first awoke, he had lived only for God and had been reared on the Talmud...dedicated to the Eternal."

But then, during the Holocaust, he watched "his mother, a beloved little sister, and all his family except his father disappear into an oven fed with living creatures." He watched the slow agony of his father's tortured death from exposure, exhaustion, and dysentery after a merciless midwinter march from Gleiwitz to Buchenwald.

"Never..., Wiesel wrote," "Never shall I forget those moments which murdered my God and turned my dreams to dust."

No one who has read *Night* can forget Wiesel's description of the scene in which the Gestapo hanged a small child.

> For more than half an hour he stayed there, struggling between life and death, dying in slow agony under our eyes. And we had to look him full in the face. He was still alive when I passed in front of him. His tongue was still red, his eyes not yet glazed.
>
> Behind me I heard a man asking, "Where is God now?"
>
> And I head a voice within me answer him: "Where is He? Here He is. He is hanging there on the gallows." [Elie Wiesel, *Night* (New York, Hill and Wang, 1958), p. 65, e book edition.]

Out of the broken pieces of his life and his faith, Elie Wiesel has forged a remarkable career ranking him among the greats of Jewish history. It earned him, among many honors, the Nobel Peace Prize in 1986. He may have stopped believing in God; but acted as though a God of love, mercy, and justice, were watching and judging his every action.

The Talmud (Kiddushin 40B) teaches us that we should approach Yom Kippur thinking our good deeds and our bad deeds balance each other on the scales. Therefore, we should go through life alert for the opportunities to perform good deeds that will tip the scales in our favor. Who knows what the impact of that next mitzvah will be?

Once, a rabbi was missing from his synagogue on the holiest night of the year. The worried elders searched for him all over town. Eventually, they found him in a small house close to the synagogue. He held a baby in his arms.

"What are you doing here?" the dumbfounded elders asked the rabbi.

"On my way to *Kol Nidre* services, I heard a baby crying. Seeing no one in the house, I stopped to comfort him."

For Jews, what we do is more important than what we believe or how we pray. Comforting a crying child is more sacred act than reciting the holiest of prayers.

As Rabbi Max Gross told Michael Kind, "About God, you don't know and I don't know, but it is in the nature of human beings to make a choice."

Personally, my choice is for God. My faith strengthens me in times of trouble; my faith enhances life's joys. For me, faith in God is a precious gift.

That gift, though, is not one that everyone has or wants. But even for those who do not believe, the Jewish holy day of Yom Kippur holds hope and promise.

Even if we do not believe in God, we can choose to act *k'eeloo* ("as if") we do.

Even if we do not believe in God, we can act as if our fate rested on the merit of our actions.

And even if we do not believe in God, we can choose life and blessing for ourselves and for others, and that is the choice that really matters.

Stephen Lewis Fuchs

CONCLUSION

The Meaning of the Journey

I hope that the journey we have taken from the Creation to the edge of the Promised Land is one that touches each of our hearts and affects how we act in the world. Our tradition teaches that God creates each one of us in the divine image. That means that each of us has talents and abilities that, if we use them properly, can make a positive difference in our world.

To be sure, we cannot all bring about world peace, cure cancer, become great athletes, actors, or scientists; but we all can do something positive to make a difference. Poverty, homelessness, hunger, pain, and the destruction of our environment, as well as loneliness, violence, and neglect, all are alive and well. Our journey bids us to seek and find a way, however small, to make this broken world a better place.

The Torah, as we have come to understand it, teaches that happiness is not the goal toward which we should aim in life. Rather, happiness and satisfaction should be by-products of living a life of purpose and meaning. In short, God calls each of us in different ways—but it is our choice whether to listen—to use our talents to forge a more just, caring, and compassionate society.

That has been God's goal for us since the time of the Creation.

Stephen Lewis Fuchs

ABOUT THE AUTHOR

After graduating high school in East Orange, New Jersey, Rabbi Stephen Fuchs graduated from Hamilton College in Clinton, New York. Post-graduation, he earned a Master's Degree in Hebrew Letters, a graduate certificate in Jewish Communal Service, and was ordained a Rabbi at Hebrew Union College in Cincinnati, Ohio. In 1992, he received a Doctor of Ministry degree in biblical interpretation at Vanderbilt University Divinity School, Nashville, Tennessee. In March 1999, he was awarded a Doctor of Divinity Degree, Honoris Causa, from the Hebrew Union College-Jewish Institute of Religion in New York.

Accomplishments

- 1987 - Meeting with Pope John Paul II with Jewish leaders in Miami, Florida.
- 1993 and 1997 - Breakfast with President and Mrs. Clinton and Vice President and Mrs. Gore at the White House.
- 1973-86 - First full-time Rabbi, Temple Isaiah, Columbia, Maryland.
- 1986-97 - Senior Rabbi, Congregation Ohabai Sholom, Nashville, Tennessee.
- 1997-2011 - Senior Rabbi of Congregation Beth Israel, West Hartford, Connecticut.
- 2011-12 - President of the World Union for Progressive Judaism. The World Union is the umbrella organization representing 1.8 million Jews in 47 countries and 1200 communities worldwide. On behalf of the World Union, Rabbi Fuchs visited more than 65 communities on five continents advocating Reform Jewish values and legitimacy.
- Fall 2013 - Interim Rabbi, Congregation Beth Shalom, Milan, Italy, with professional visits to Florence and Turin.
- Fall 2014 - Served Reform congregations in northern Germany and worked with Lutheran Church to foster inter-religious

understanding.

Rabbi Stephen Fuchs has also been:

- President of the Greater Hartford Rabbinical Association.
- Chair of the Central Conference of American Rabbis' Committee on Inter-religious Affairs.
- Trustee of the Hartford Seminary, a Trustee of Saint Francis Hospital, the Hartford Rotary Club, and the Anti Defamation League of B'nai Brith Regional Board of Connecticut.
- Adjunct Professor at Hartford Seminary.
- Adjunct Professor at the University of Saint Joseph, West Hartford, Connecticut.
- Adjunct Professor at the Lutheran Theological Seminary in Philadelphia.
- Lecturer on Genesis Earliest Stories at Hamilton College Elder Hostel program.

Awards

- 2004 - First Annual Judaic Heritage Award, presented by The Charter Oak Cultural Center.
- 2006 - The Four Chaplains Award for service to the community beyond religious boundaries.
- 2011 - Unlimited Love Humanitarian Award presented by Bethel Center Humane Services.

Rabbi Fuchs has written and lectured extensively and published more than 100 articles, essays, and book chapters on subjects pertaining to Jewish life, Israel, and inter-religious relations.

Throughout Rabbi Fuchs' career, he has undertaken major social campaigns to foster dialogue and understanding. For several years he was one of the co-chairs of the Interfaith Fellowship for Universal Health Care. This group was instrumental in securing the passage of the 2009 SustiNet legislation to provide quality affordable health care for the residents of Connecticut.

Rabbi Fuchs has also spoken out from the pulpit, in public lectures, on TV, radio, and in the press about the harmful impact on young people of the proliferation of graphic violence in movies, video games, and TV programs.

At Congregation Beth Israel, Rabbi Fuchs annually facilitated the largest synagogue food drive in the country for the Yom Kippur Food Drive. Connecticut FOODSHARE created and named a special food-transportation fund in honor of Rabbi Fuchs.

"I see the essence of Jewish values expressed in concrete acts of caring and kindness that make a difference in the lives of others."

Happily married for over 40 years to Victoria, a retired elementary school teacher, Rabbi Fuchs is the proud father of Leo, Sarah, and Benjamin, and father-in-law to Liz, Dan and Kristin, as well as the devoted grandfather of Zachary, Micah, Jeremy, Noa, and Flora. Rabbi Fuchs is an avid reader, crossword puzzle solver, and tennis player. During college summers, he worked as both the Assistant Tennis Pro at the famed Concord Hotel in the Catskills and as the Head Pro at Spring Garden Country Club in Florham Park, New Jersey.

Stephen Lewis Fuchs

CONTACT THE AUTHOR

In addition to book signings, Rabbi Fuchs is available for speaking engagements, presentations, and group discussions to provide further insight into the message and topics covered in *What's in It for Me?* He speaks at synagogues, churches, corporate and civic meetings, book clubs, and other groups, large and small.

Thank you for reading my book. If you found *What's in It for Me?* meaningful, I would be so grateful if you wrote a reader review on Amazon!

Rabbi Stephen Fuchs

To book an engagement, please contact him at meinbiblicalnarratives@gmail.com.

Visit his webpage: www.rabbifuchs.com